With some of my Sikh friends in Hamilton.

I always enjoy meeting young Canadians.

Chatting with young Prince William.

Austin (centre) and I share a joke with Prince Charles.

To Mom:

From one Feminist to another... hehe! Have a Merry Christmas!

Love Laura

Christmas 2004

SHEILA
COPPS

WORTH FIGHTING FOR

⌈A DOUGLAS GIBSON BOOK⌉

M&S

Library and Archives Canada Cataloguing in Publication

Copps, Sheila, 1952-
Worth fighting for / Sheila Copps.

ISBN 0-7710-2282-4

1. Copps, Sheila, 1952-   2. Canada–Politics and government–1984-1993.
3. Canada–Politics and government–1993-   4. Ontario–Politics and
government–1943-1985.   5. Martin, Paul, 1938-.   6. Cabinet
ministers–Canada–Biography. 7. Politicians–Canada–Biography.   I. Title.

FC636.C66A3 2004   971.064'8   C2004-904195-9

We acknowledge the financial support of the Government of Canada through the Book Publishing Industry Development Program and that of the Government of Ontario through the Ontario Media Development Corporation's Ontario Book Initiative. We further acknowledge the support of the Canada Council for the Arts and the Ontario Arts Council for our publishing program.

Typeset in Bembo by M&S, Toronto
Printed and bound in Canada

A Douglas Gibson Book

This book is printed on acid-free paper that is 100% recycled,
ancient-forest friendly (100% post-consumer recycled).

McClelland & Stewart Ltd.
The Canadian Publishers
481 University Avenue
Toronto, Ontario
M5G 2E9
www.mcclelland.com

1 2 3 4 5   08 07 06 05 04

To my mother and father who taught me the power of truth. To my sailor, Austin, who led me through the narrows to the ocean of life and politics. To my daughter, Danelle, who shared me with the country for 17 years. To my stepchildren, Jackie, Sue, and Steve, who taught me that sharing love makes it grow. To my grandchildren, who make us realize why democracy counts.

Contents

Foreword

I am very pleased to write the Foreword to this book by Sheila Copps. Sheila is an old friend, a colleague for many years, and a true Liberal. I have always admired her dedicated hard work and her loyalty.

Sheila has always been outspoken; it is one of her most notable characteristics. If you ask Sheila for her opinion, you will get it, even if you don't always like what you hear!

I have found that life around Sheila is never dull, and her account of her life in politics is sure to find many interested readers all over Canada.

Since her election to Parliament in 1984 she has worked hard and very effectively as a very good MP and an excellent Minister and Deputy Prime Minister. In these roles, she has given our country great service, and I wish her – and her book – every success.

Jean Chrétien
August, 2004

Introduction

In her first book, *Nobody's Baby*, written in 1986, Sheila wrote that she "didn't intend to stay in politics for a lifetime," which at the time caused me to feel some relief. Little did she know then that in 2004 she would end up as "nobody's baby" in fact - as a result of her abandonment by her leader Paul Martin, who left her as a political foundling on the doorstep of Hamilton East where she had been for eighteen years their MP.

I write this Introduction to her new book as a tribute to a feisty, sometimes ferocious, feminist protagonist, never shy or retiring but personable and prickly, never demure but attention-getting and with a redoubtable political personality. She was a constant thorn in my side while she was in Opposition, but her marriage to my fellow Newfoundlander Austin Thorne has made her more serene and has calmed her sometimes volcanic and partisan excesses.

In her early parliamentary days of the first Mulroney administration, she was a member of the infamous Rat Pack of Tobin, Nunziata, Boudria, and Copps, the rodent brigade of the Turner caucus. Who could forget Sheila's pursuit of Sinclair Stevens at a committee hearing on the exaggerated conflict-of-interest allegations against Sinc when Sheila jumped over furniture in a single bound, outdoing Superman in her outrage and derision?

I regret that she didn't object in similar fashion to Finance Minister Martin ignoring for years the rules that should have prevented what to this outsider (and former finance minister) looks like a massive conflict of interest, with the owner of Canada Steamship Lines apparently benefiting from decisions made by his own department!

In the case of Sheila, Paul Martin did nothing to resolve the conflict over her nomination in Hamilton East.

Never afraid to express her views and give her opinions, she was one of the feminist Four Horsewomen of the Apocalypse with Judy Rebick, Mary Clancey, and Dawn Black, dubbed by the *Montreal Gazette* as "My Unerotic Nightmares" and by the *Globe and Mail* as "The Four Horsewomen of the Apocalypse, namely famine, pestilence, war, and the National Action Committee on the Status of Women." She will certainly be missed, not least by me. A woman of ability, an able minister, colourful and forthright, sympathetic to the underdog, her book reflects all of these characteristics.

Now absent from official politics, Sheila is one of the numerous Canadians adversely affected by the truth of the observation of Lord Acton that "Power tends to corrupt; absolute power corrupts absolutely." An English wit's amended version suits even better those now in control of the Liberal Party, especially Paul Martin, that "Power is delightful and absolute power is absolutely delightful."

In the somewhat dull and boring world of Canadian politics, Sheila is a bright light, sometimes voluble and gaudy, but always herself. She will be back, and always welcomed by those who enjoy forthrightness, enthusiasm, strong opinions, and outrageous actions.

Finally:

I regret that Ms. Sheila Copps,
Doesn't always appreciate my bon motts,
Gets feminist's fits
At my sexist bits,
And very irate
When I don't act straight,
Doesn't drink my tequila
But hollers and squeala's.
I hope she'll accept my new peace feelers…
And I recommend her book to all book dealers.

John C. Crosbie
St. John's, August, 2004

Chapter One

On the Hill

The ides of March came a little early this year. March 6 was the day that marked a turning point in my lifelong devotion to the Liberal Party of Canada. March 6 was the day I lost a bitter nomination battle to become the Liberal candidate in Hamilton East–Stoney Creek. I didn't pick the date. It was chosen by Prime Minister Paul Martin's chief political operative in Ontario, Karl Littler. You should know that in party circles Karl has another moniker. They called him, with considerable overstatement, Karl Hitler. Karl was one of the closest associates of Paul Martin during the years he was working toward the top job. He worked alongside David Herle, another close Martin ally who had started on Paul Martin's payroll before he even entered politics.

Herle knew what an obsessive compaigner Littler was. According to Susan Delacourt in her book *Juggernaut: Paul Martin's Campaign for Chrétien's Crown*, in the summer of 2002, "Herle joked that Littler was the Colonel Kurtz in this *Heart of Darkness* drama; even when the campaign ended, Littler would remain at large, fighting for the cause."

Along with Terrie O'Leary and Mike Robinson, David Herle and Karl Littler were the brains trust behind Paul Martin's rise to power. Or should I say, brains and brawn. They often seemed more brawn than brains. Karl earned his nickname by his street brawling behaviour in the backrooms working on Paul Martin's behalf in the years leading up to Prime Minister Martin's ascendance in early 2004 to the job he had coveted for twenty years.

"Covet" is a pretty strong word for a sin that's mentioned in two of the Ten Commandments. "Thou shall not covet thy neighbour's wife." "Thou shall not covet thy neighbour's goods," and so on. But covetousness in politics is part of the package, just as drive and ambition are necessary prerequisites to survive in the political world in Ottawa.

I first got wind of Paul Martin's prime-ministerial ambition on a night of disaster for the Liberals, September 4, 1984. It was the eve of the Mulroney landslide. We knew that things were looking bad. I was in my Hamilton East headquarters putting the finishing touches on the voters' list, getting out the vote that would ensure our survival. As we worked furiously into the night, trying to stave off certain defeat, the phone rang. It was Dennis Dawson on the line from Quebec City asking how things were going. I didn't really know Dennis, except as one of our candidates, and after thanking him for the courtesy call, I asked him why he wasn't working in his own riding in Quebec. "If I don't win this election," he said, "there won't be a Liberal dogcatcher elected in the province of Quebec."

The next day as the results poured in, he was pretty nearly right. In fact there were only forty Liberals elected across the country – ten new faces and thirty shell-shocked veterans. When the final count was in, I was the only Liberal elected between Toronto and Windsor. Dennis lost, so I didn't think I would hear from him again, but within a couple of months, I received a phone call from him. His friend Paul Martin was going to be in Ottawa and he would like to meet with me. A meeting was set up early in the new year of 1985, a drink at the Rideau Club, long a watering hole for business and political types in the nation's capital, with a bust of Sir John A. in the lobby and a history that is pre-Confederation. The drink was pleasant, but brief. Mr. Martin made it very clear that the reason for the meeting was that he wanted to pursue the twin objectives of becoming a member of Parliament and then prime minister. At the time I remember thinking his ambition was admirable but wondered if his business experience in the world of Montreal dockyards could translate into the bridge-building skills required to be a politician. I didn't spend a lot of time worrying about Paul Martin's future in public life because I was busy trying to find my own way in the amazing political labyrinth called Parliament Hill.

When I decided to run in 1984 I had very little time to reflect on what life in the nation's capital might be like. My predecessor in Hamilton East, John Munro, had resigned from public life after running unsuccessfully against John Turner and Jean Chrétien for the leadership. I had supported John in the leadership and we were both cut from the same cloth. John always fought, and fought hard, for the little person. If John was your friend, you had a friend for life; if he was your enemy, watch out. In fact, in 1976, John's friendly generosity saved my mother from the poorhouse. My dad had become a very successful local politician in Hamilton, elected consecutively for sixteen years before he was felled by a heart attack while running in a marathon in March 1976. He suffered massive brain damage from anoxia and was in a semi-comatose state for six weeks. When he left the hospital, he could never work again and his pension totalled $160 a month. John Munro immediately got to work. He and friends organized a "Thanks Vic" Day in my father's honour. They held a sold-out dinner and also peddled "THANKS VIC" buttons at a special Ticats game in his honour. They raised $170,000, which was put into a trust fund for my mother. But that wasn't enough for John. He arranged for my mother to be named as a citizenship judge, a position she held until Brian Mulroney tossed her out ten years later. John was that kind of person. He would work his heart out for a cause he believed in. Often misunderstood at the national level, he was revered in Hamilton for the quality of perseverance that seems to be bred in steel-making communities. We never give up.

John had announced his desire to step aside just before the writ was issued in 1984, which gave me very little time to make my decision. Should I vacate a provincial seat that I had held for less than a full term? Did I really know what I was getting into? I remember at one point waking up in the middle of the night in a cold sweat asking myself "What have you done?" It got worse. In what could only be described as a disastrous national campaign, we started dropping three points a day and I wondered whether I would ever make it to Parliament. Had I made the right decision in leaving the Provincial legislature in Toronto, where I felt at home, to take my chances in Ottawa?

I still remember the day I arrived in Ottawa. I stood at the bottom of Parliament Hill (and it really is a hill) and looked up to the place where I would be working. The eternal flame flickering in front of the gothic towers of the Parliament buildings; a picture of inspiration and idealism. I was awed, and at the same time I felt at home. Twenty years later, when I drove my Liberal-red sports car away on the last day of the parliamentary session, I still felt the same mix of emotions.

The Rat Pack

My first few years in Ottawa swept by quickly. From 1984 to 1988 we were in survival mode. Many pundits were predicting the death of the Liberal Party, suggesting that Canada would abandon the notion of a centrist Liberal Party and follow the political trends of most other modern democracies, producing a clear split between parties of the right and the left. Liberalism was dead, trumpeted most eminent political watchers. In future, they announced with great confidence, Canada would follow the lead of most other nations with a pitched battle between the left and the right and the Liberal Party would be a casualty of the middle ground. Ed Broadbent had just taken the New Democratic Party to their highest support ever and Brian Mulroney's crushing victory did not leave a lot of room for the Grits.

From the depths of annihilation, however, emerged the Rat Pack, named by *Toronto Star* reporter Joe O'Donnell after the Hollywood Brat Pack. We had six members. Four English, two French, and most of us with previous political experience at city hall or in provincial legislatures. There was John Nunziata, a feisty former Toronto City Councillor; Don Boudria, a former municipal politician in Cumberland; and Brian Tobin, a media whiz with political experience in his native Newfoundland. From Quebec we were joined by Jean Lapierre, an André Ouellet protégé who served briefly in John Turner's cabinet, and Jean-Claude Malepart, a street fighter from the east end of Montreal. Our job, as we saw it, was to fight for social justice and against Brian Mulroney, and to use whatever tactics were necessary.

John Nunziata had experience as a lawyer and a municipal politician. He was intelligent, aggressive, and unrelenting. He was also not afraid to swim against the stream. In fact he almost relished it. If he was on your side, you had a winner. If not, keep your head up, and your elbows.

Don Boudria was a true Horatio Alger story. After dropping out of high school, Don got his first job as a dishwasher on Parliament Hill. He rose through the ranks by sheer hard work to eventually become the minister responsible for running the place, and in his spare time got his university degree. Don was the quintessential constituency man. He read every piece of correspondence himself and guaranteed a forty-eight-hour turnaround time on all constituent phone calls. Little wonder that when he became the government leader in the House, he had everything scrupulously annotated by subject matter. Don was proud to be thorough and cherished the nickname "binder boy" pinned on him by MP Deborah Grey during a raucous Question Period exchange.

As for Brian Tobin, he rose from the ranks of the media, and it showed. He had an uncanny ability to smell a story a mile away and his savvy in television and marketing was a joy to behold. He knew how to draw pictures with words and images. Probably one of the most brilliant flashpoints of our time in government was Brian Tobin on the docks in New York holding up a fisherman's net and explaining how those "last living little turbots" were hanging on by their fingernails on the Grand Banks. It mattered little that a metaphor was mangled. The Spaniards didn't have a chance against those tiny fish. That was the day he won the Turbot War.

In a sense, Jean Lapierre was the French equivalent of Brian Tobin. He had an uncanny flair for knowing the story and he had so many friends in the media that he rendered the NDP invisible in his home province in a matter of weeks.

Social activist Jean-Claude Malepart was larger than life in every sense of the word. Jean-Claude knew all the players in Quebec and he could easily organize a Parliament Hill demonstration with two days' notice. In fact, he was the one who brought the little lady to Parliament Hill who ambushed Prime Minister Mulroney with the famous "you're a liar, Charlie Brown" quote over a reduction in old-age pensions.

We were six among forty members in the Liberal caucus, including ten new members, sandwiched in between the NDP, led by the eloquent Ed Broadbent, and the governing Tories, with a prime minister swept in by the largest majority in Canadian history, 211 seats. Our caucus was bruised and divided. Veterans like Lloyd Axworthy and André Ouellet, both of whom were among the smartest politicians I have ever met, believed that since the voters had spoken in such great numbers, it would be wise for us to go on automatic pilot for at least twelve months and leave the opposing to the NDP. They thought the country would have no appetite for the Liberal Party until we had spent sufficient time in political purgatory to earn the right to speak. Many other Liberals agreed with this plan of keeping a low profile. Then there was the Rat Pack. John Nunziata and I had both had considerable experience fighting the NDP in our own constituencies. It was our view that if we did not mount a spirited attack on the government of the day, our job would be done by the NDP and *they* would become the de facto official opposition. So our objective was not only to expose the government, but also to ensure that the real opposition was the Liberal Party.

We accomplished that task by old-fashioned investigative legwork. Soon anonymous brown envelopes were arriving every day, but to ensure that we had solid research behind us we used the principles I had learned at the University of Western Ontario in Journalism 101. We needed two solid sources behind every story, and we had to answer the five Ws: who, what, when, where, and why. The last principle was "KISS": Keep it Simple, Sheila.

We also remembered one of the fundamental tenets of politics: Have fun. A Rat Pack T-shirt was created which we unabashedly sold at Liberal fundraisers. Because Fridays are always a dull day in the House of Commons, we created the Friday Award, which was also named the PAW award (Patronage Award of the Week). Every Friday it was given by the Rat Pack, with a lot of flourish and rhetoric, to the Conservative who had best dined at the trough that week.

We also included hard-edged investigative research, working effectively with journalists to expose incompetence or dishonesty in the Conservative cabinet. In one year our list of victims was long, from the questionable decisions around the sale of tainted tuna approved by the Minister of Fisheries, John Fraser, to the exposure of Sinclair Stevens to the Parker Inquiry for mixing business and politics. In between was the mussels scandal that affected Health Minister Jake Epp, a toxic mess that left dozens of Canadians with permanent brain damage after they ate bad mussels. Then there was the strange relationship between minister Stuart McGinnis and his former broker, a man he appointed to a government agency responsible for making investments. I received a tip that there was some hanky-panky going on regarding the minister's blind trust. I remember at one point stating, on an Atlantic television program, that I would put my seat on the line if the minister could provide a proper blind-trust document. He could not and I did not have to resign my seat, but it was a precursor of another promise I made on television regarding another matter of honour called the GST.

As we planned our Question-Period strategy, we worked as a team. When a minister was bloodied by one questioner, the next would go in for the kill with a tough follow-up. We were organized, sustained, bilingual, and backed by great researchers. But sometimes in our quest for the kill we forgot the big picture. For example, I now regret the gusto with which we attacked what we called "Tunagate." We even had a Christmas board game made in a tuna can that sold as a stocking stuffer at the annual Liberal Christmas party. I still remember the very honest and cerebral Warren Allmand, a former solicitor-general, coming to the preparation session for Question Period and arguing that the Honourable John Fraser was a decent man who did not deserve to be destroyed by our pillorying. He even begged Herb Gray to drop us off the Question Period. We were unflinching, insisting that the truth was more important, and ultimately Mr. Gray allowed us to keep asking questions. John Fraser did step down, but it was a testament to his popularity that he was later elected Speaker and became one of the most effective in parliamentary history. As I came to know him, I realized that Warren Allmand had been right. Sometimes, in our desire to get the facts out, we forgot the human element – and that, after all, is what politics should be about.

The list of transgressing Tories continued: Suzanne Blais-Grenier, Andrée Champagne, Michel Côté, André Bissonnette. Within two years, the Mulroney government was reeling from allegations of corruption, most of them directly tied to the incessant badgering by the Rat Pack in Question Period.

Pursuing Sinclair Stevens

The most infamous Sheila Copps scene etched in the minds of Canadians from those days is of me jumping over a table to get at a fleeing witness. In fact it never happened. It was in a committee where the infamous showdown with Sinclair Stevens occurred. Mr. Stevens had been called by the committee to explain the seeming conflict of interest between the selling of strip bonds and papal coins and his role as minister responsible for industry. At the time he tried to argue that the business activities were those of his spouse and therefore not linked to him. He was subsequently found in breach on several counts of conflict of interest in an inquiry by Justice Parker established by Brian Mulroney.

This particular evening the committee was holding hearings in a tiny, cramped West Block committee room crawling with dozens of journalists and cameras. We were all frustrated by Mr. Stevens' stonewalling. When the Tory chairman deemed the meeting over, Mr. Stevens, accompanied by André Bissonnette (a huge man towering well over six feet), headed for the door to avoid further questions. I, however, reverted to my old sports background, climbing on a chair to get past the packed crowd that ringed the outside of the room, and making my way to the door to confront him on the way out. There I was grabbed by the neck and shoved up against the wall by Mr. Bissonnette as Mr. Stevens slunk by. As we pursued him down the hallway, Mr. Stevens jumped into a waiting car, leaving Mr. Bissonnette to fend for himself against Mr. Nunziata. The news highlighted the event as a sort of Hockey Night in Canada and thereafter I was pilloried as the woman who had "jumped over tables" to get at Sinclair Stevens. No mention was ever made of the assault by Bissonnette. Even John Nunziata's spirited pursuit on the front lawn of the House of Commons was overshadowed by the fact that I had climbed on a chair to pursue my political prey.

At the end of the evening, we gathered in the office of Marcel Prudhomme, then a long-serving Liberal member of Parliament. We watched the eleven o'clock news with horror, realizing the issue of the fraud was being overshadowed by the acrobatics of a committee meeting. Mr. Stevens had recently experienced heart problems and we were deathly afraid he might be admitted to hospital that night and nicely exit the whole mess. He did not, and we lived to fight another day. In the end, the issues of conflict of interest were well established in the Parker Inquiry, which led to the creation of a whole new code of conduct for ministers.

What shocked me most about the incident was the blatant, unthinking sexism of the Press Gallery. Here you had a parliamentary secretary to a minister (male) and another male opposition member roughing it up, and yet to see the headlines you would think I had been at the meeting by myself. For years, I was known as the woman who leapt over tables to get at a Minister; the member who grabbed me by the neck was not part of the story.

In the beginning, I was absolutely appalled by the level of stereotyping in the media, but through the years I came to understand that the preponderance of white, male faces in the Gallery did not encourage diversity of opinion. To make matters worse, they did not see any sexism. In the last twenty years Canada has changed dramatically. Demographically, it's clear that we are not the country we were twenty years ago. But a stroll through the halls of power will show you that not much has changed there. In fact most of the reporters who were in Ottawa when I started are still writing, and many of them see no need for their ranks to be replenished by the new ideas that would come from different perspectives on gender and diversity. Ironically, the concentration of coverage on Belinda Stronach's bid to become the Leader of her party focused on how she dressed and the fact that she was, as one newspaper put it on their front page, "Blonde Ambition." Stephen Harper is blond as well, but nobody would dare refer to him by his hair colour. Yet in 2004 the double standard applied to men and women is alive and well in politics and journalism.

All that to say that during the time of the Rat Pack my image was established as a shrill, even screaming, political moll whose take-no-prisoners attitude was definitely beyond the bounds of Parliament Hill politeness. But our approach was also dictated by the fact that the NDP was breathing down our necks, and many of the pundits were predicting the death of Liberalism. So our approach was to fight hard to keep the Liberal Party alive, even in the headlines, at a time when most Liberals were taking a political sabbatical recovering from the drubbing we had taken at the hands of the Tories in the 1984 election.

As John Gray put it in his biography, *Paul Martin: The Power of Ambition*: "There were days in the Commons when it seemed there was nothing between Turner and invisibility except the Rat Pack. Elegant they were not, noisy and effective they were."

Chapter Two
_____

A Political Education

The twenty years leading up to 1984 were very good years for Liberals. With the rare exception of a series of by-elections in 1978 and the brief flirtation with Joe Clark's Tory minority in 1979, Liberalism was in. Not only was Liberalism in but the country was coming of age. Centennial year, 1967, was a time for all Canadians to be optimistic about the future. Ironically, although I was just a high-school kid from Hamilton, I was in Montreal during two events which really shaped Canadian history. First, when Charles de Gaulle gave his famous speech I was visiting Expo with my family. My father, who spoke fluent French, was good friends with Mayor Jean Drapeau and had even convinced the Quebec Association of Municipalities to rejoin the Federation of Canadian Municipalities when he sat as president. I remember my mother's furious reaction to General de Gaulle's "Vive le Québec libre." She told my startled father that she would like to take a gun and shoot the French president. That emotional statement by a loyal Canadian (with no background as a sniper) was a foretaste of the visceral emotions that would characterize the fight for Canada, draining our country of vital energy that could, and should, have gone elsewhere.

In the same year, I was in Montreal playing in a basketball tournament the weekend Pierre Trudeau was elected Leader of the Liberal Party. Ironically, my father was at the convention supporting Paul Martin Sr. Their common ties through the Knights of Columbus and their shared roots in the Ottawa Valley were what bound them together. Although my father was born in Haileybury and raised in Timmins, Ontario, his parents hailed from Eganville, the heart of expatriate Catholic Irish territory and close to the parental birthplace of Paul Martin Sr. in Pembroke. While I was catching snippets of the Liberal convention on television, my basketball teammates were far more interested in the fun of Montreal. They could not fathom my fascination with the Liberal convention in general and Pierre Trudeau in particular. To me Trudeau personified youth and savvy at the same time. His charisma almost literally leapt through the television screen in the rundown Montreal motel room housing our girls' team.

We went on to win the tournament and that same girls' team gets together for beer and reminiscing thirty-six years later. In fact, I am still dragging the team to the occasional political gig. They come out of friendship but they still wonder why I am as obsessed about politics as we were about basketball those many decades ago at Bishop Ryan High School. Even in those days, basketball and politics was a necessary mix. I led my first strike when the girls' team could not get enough gym time because the boys had bumping rights, even though they were out of the championships and we were in contention. When I put together a group to go see our principal, Father Côté, he agreed the girls were being short-changed and ordered a change in schedules, giving the girls' and boys' teams equal time in the gym. That was in 1966. So with that sort of grassroots political involvement behind me, it was maybe not a total surprise to the team that I would be obsessed with Pierre Trudeau the following year.

I had a chance to witness Trudeau's charisma first-hand in 1982. I had been elected to the provincial legislature in Ontario in 1981 and within a year was in a leadership race against David Peterson. David hailed from London, Ontario. He was a funny, bright lawyer who was smart enough to solidify the right wing of the party in his bid to become the leader. My campaign consisted of emphasizing key Liberal issues like bilingualism and the inclusion of sexual orientation as a core issue in the human rights code of the province. David was astute enough to realize that he would have to campaign from the right to solidify support in Orange Ontario and become the first Liberal premier in almost fifty years. Through the years, David and I remained good friends and I came to appreciate his solid principles and openness to all. But in those days, I was trying to beat him. I had scored a real coup when Keith Davey, the Liberal "Rainmaker," agreed to set up a meeting with Mr. Trudeau. Keith was probably one of the most brilliant minds in politics; hence his nickname, because he could make it rain votes. The fact that he was promoting me for provincial leader gave my campaign a much-needed boost in credibility. I was young, twenty-nine, impressionable, and in awe to find myself ushered into the office of the prime minister, rich with burnished oak and history.

To my surprise, the Prime Minister did not seem very interested in my political views; instead he was fascinated to know why a young, attractive woman like me would be interested in, or, as he put it wanted to "waste her time" in politics. As we talked, our meeting time surpassed the allotted fifteen minutes and when I left the forty-five-minute meeting the connection had been more personal than anything else. At the same time, when he spoke about his vision for Canada and his hope for outward-looking world citizenship embracing diversity, he put the meaning of politics on a higher plane. I could definitely see how his charm attracted women voters by the millions. His lidded eyes and veiled smile left me with the impression that there was a lot more to discover in the man than any forty-five-minute interlude could reveal. I guess that was his secret – he always left people waiting for, and wanting, more.

His interest was not in the tactics of politics. That was left to mere mortals like Jimmy Coutts and Keith Davey. Keith Davey examined all the political angles and Jim Coutts kept the Prime Minister's operation running flawlessly. They were an incredibly successful duo. In later years, Coutts would try his hand at active politics. I remember joining him to campaign for a seat in the recent vacancy in Toronto–Spadina created when Peter Stollery was elevated to the Senate. Joyce Fairbairn, another Trudeau intimate who had worked in communications for the Prime Minister, joined us as we knocked on door after door in the by-election, only to have many of them slammed in our faces. It was quite a different experience from running the Prime Minister's Office, but Coutts was unflappable. You could quickly see why he and Davey were such a brilliant team, leaving the Prime Minister free to think about the world.

Prime Minister Trudeau was never very interested in the rough-and-tumble world of party politics. His was a higher calling, almost a monastic one. He didn't worry about the politics of winning, but left those campaign strategies and tactical manoeuvres to a good team. He thought bigger. His vision was of a Canada secure in her place in the world because she was secure in herself, with a Charter of Rights and Freedoms to ensure that the majority could not trump the minority, with a multicultural commitment to shape a country where monoculturalism was shunned. He gave us the first negotiating table that included aboriginal peoples. In fact, it was his vision that gave us the Canada of the late twentieth century. When he sped off in his Mercedes in the spring of 1984, the usual list of pundits produced the usual list of grievances. They did not see the seeds he had planted.

But the people saw. That was why, upon his death sixteen years later, thousands of people lined up for hours in Ottawa and Montreal to pay him homage by filing silently past his coffin. That was why the rail line that carried his body and his grieving sons to Montreal was dotted all the way along its length with thousands of Canadians saying their last goodbyes. That was why, notwithstanding the years of pounding he had taken from the separatists, the ordinary people lined up in front of the Cathedral in Montreal just to get a last glimpse of a man who had shaped the new Canada.

Ironically, he may have been warmly embraced by the people, yet even after his death, some political elites in Quebec could not quite open their hearts to him. You may not have noticed that before the funeral the former prime minister lay in state at Montreal's City Hall and not at Notre Dame Cathedral. As Minister of Canadian Heritage, I was responsible for organizing the Ottawa and Montreal ceremonies and I know the reason why. The cardinal responsible for booking the Cathedral, Cardinal Turcotte, ever the politically correct Quebecer, somehow could not arrange to clear the cathedral for a Prime Minister of Canada because that would have meant rearranging a concert. A couple of years later, the same cardinal had no problem organizing a quasi-state funeral for Pierre Bourgault, a rabid separatist. In the topsy-turvy world of Quebec politics, being a federalist and a Prime Minister was enough to deny Pierre Trudeau, a devout Catholic, the full services of the cathedral for his burial. During Mr. Trudeau's funeral, I listened in vain for the word "Canadian" or "Canada" in the cardinal's eulogy. It was left to Justin Trudeau to overcome the cardinal's grudging words.

My first experience with a political funeral actually came even before I entered federal politics. I was a newly minted provincial member of the legislative assembly and the well-respected former premier John Robarts had died an early death of his own choosing after a severe stroke had left him without speech (obviously a living hell for such an articulate person). In his latter years Mr. Robarts had married a much younger, attractive woman. His funeral, a stately affair at St. James's Cathedral in Toronto, drew the crème de la crème of Canadian political life. Mr. Trudeau, as prime minister, was there along with several other Canadian political icons. I was sandwiched in between provincial colleagues Robert Nixon and Sean Conway. Bob is the father of federal minister Jane Stewart, and like Jane, he had a great sense of humour and a real zest for life. (Even in death.) As Mrs. Robarts walked into the church behind the casket of her late husband, she was supported by the

Prime Minister, who steadied her on his arm. Mr. Nixon, noticing her dependence on Mr. Trudeau, leaned over to the rest of us and whispered a wry comment about it with a grin. I remember being genuinely surprised at the time that everyone's thoughts were not all devoted to respectful memories of Mr. Robarts. In retrospect I came to realize that Mr. Nixon's comments were better examples of the kind of backroom chatter that goes on in Parliament and in funeral parlours; in those days, I was young and naive. More than two decades later, nothing surprises me. In fact, following the untimely death in the spring of 2004 of my provincial colleague and friend, MPP Dominic Agostino, there was another example. Dominic wasn't even buried before friends were calling to suggest I assume the vacancy in Hamilton East created by his death and thus avoid the embarrassment to the Liberal Party that an appeal of my rigged nomination process might engender.

Power and Influence

After all these years I think I may have an answer to Pierre Trudeau's question about what drew me to politics. Money was not the motivator. Then what about power? There's no doubt that power is perhaps the least understood part of politics. Much is written about the power of the Prime Minister's Office, the power of cabinet ministers, and so on. And yet there are MPs who can never reasonably expect to sit in cabinet for whom the aphrodisiac of politics is every bit as compelling. Tommy Douglas never sat in cabinet and yet today's single most defining Canadian creation, Medicare, sprang from his party and its time in office in Saskatchewan. Does this mean that his power, the power of an idea, has less longevity or credence than that of a federal minister or a prime minister? You could reasonably argue that his influence on the course of Canadian history was greater than most ministers and some prime ministers. Douglas's legacy, that of a medical system where all Canadians could be treated equally, regardless of the size of their wallet, is an enduring value that the majority of Canadians cherish today.

Most Canadians have probably never heard of Adelaide Hoodless. She was responsible for creating one of the first organizations in the world devoted to women's empowerment. Hoodless founded the first Women's Institute in Stoney Creek, Ontario, in an effort to promote the issues of the day that concerned women. She believed that through the development of women's abilities and skills, their quality of life would improve. This first institute grew to more than five hundred institutes, and some thirty thousand members.

Adelaide Hoodless began the movement to lobby for the pasteurization of milk when she lost a son who drank unpasteurized milk. The simple act of boiling the milk could have saved her son's life and yet the political authorities of the day were too immobilized by the milk production lobby to do anything about it. So Hoodless gathered a group of like-minded women and formed the Women's Institute, which ultimately used their power to influence governments to make changes to protect families and children.

What does this have to do with power and politics? The pasteurization of milk managed to save thousands of infant lives, probably more young lives than any other single government initiative in the twentieth century. Yet Canadian history texts barely mention this courageous and innovative woman. In a small way, as Canadian Heritage Minister, I tried to tell the story of true Canadian heroes through the path of the "Heroes" program, which included the story of Adelaide Hoodless.

Making the Famous Five Famous

When I first arrived in Parliament, I was fascinated by the lack of any female presence in the "halls of power." In fact, in my first year on the Hill, there was not even a women's washroom on the floor where my office was located. In the six-storey Centre Block of the Parliament buildings, it was considered only necessary to have female restrooms on alternate floors. When I roamed the halls of Parliament, replete with paintings and busts of every prime minister, every Speaker, and various political luminaries dating back to 1867, very few women were to be found. A portrait of Jeanne Sauvé, Canada's first woman Speaker, who went on to become our first female Governor-General, stood alone. Imagine my surprise when on my way to the women's washroom one day, I saw the bust of a woman's head identified as Agnes MacPhail, the first woman to enter the House of Commons. And there she was, appropriately positioned in an obscure, dark corner of the second floor, inaccessible to the public, outside the women's washroom. When I had the chance, I approached the then Speaker, John Fraser, about giving Agnes MacPhail the prominence she deserved. I asked that her bust be moved to a position of honour in front of the Chamber she so proudly served. Without hesitation, he ordered the bust moved to a more visible location, where she is now a regular part of school tours seen by thousands of children who know that their Parliament included at least one woman.

Imagine for a moment those thousands of schoolchildren who make a pilgrimage to Ottawa every year, walking through the halls of Parliament, the repository of their nation's history, to see the stories of their country unfold in pictures and words. The absence of the voices and faces of women speaks volumes about how we encourage our children to shape a future. The absence of visible minorities except as security guards is appalling. Why should the symbols of Parliament and government be anything less than the reflection of who we are and where we come from? The first black to arrive in Canada, Mathieu da Costa, actually came to these shores with Samuel de Champlain four hundred years ago. In fact, he was the translator between the explorers and the aboriginal people, and were it not for aboriginal support and da Costa's language skills, Champlain would not have survived the first bleak winter. Yet, like Mathieu, aboriginal peoples are strangely absent from the halls of Parliament, even though the buildings themselves were built on land that was taken from the Algonquin people.

It's important for people to know that the most popular statue grouping on the Hill, the "Famous Five," named after the five women who established that women were actually Persons in Canadian law (by appealing to the British Parliament, having been turned down by Canada), almost never got there.

The original "Famous Five" committee sprang out of Alberta, home to many fiery women in the early twentieth century. Some of these women decided they were tired of being defined, along with children and cattle, as the property of men under Canadian law. They decided to exercise their power and initiate a political movement to demand that women be recognized as persons in the law. They were pilloried, excoriated, and dismissed by the editorial writers of the day (plus ça change, plus c'est la même chose) for not knowing their place and quietly getting on with the womanly duties of child-rearing and housekeeping. But they persisted, and when the Canadian cabinet refused to recognize women as persons, the "Famous Five" appealed to the British House of Lords. This appeal changed the course of Canadian history. The British Parliament ruled that Canadian women were indeed persons and as such entitled to the same rights and responsibilities as men (voting, holding office, sitting in the Senate, and so on).

That case was won in 1919 and yet, seven decades later, women were rarely to be found in the symbols of governance given prominence on Parliament Hill. One rarefied example whose portrait did appear was Canada's first woman Speaker and Governor General, Jeanne Sauvé. Otherwise, as I've mentioned, there was the bust of Agnes MacPhail, Canada's first woman parliamentarian, in the back hall beside the Speaker's quarters, but there were no statues of women on the grounds of Parliament except for those of the Queen.

The "Famous Five" committee, chaired by Frances Wright of Calgary, decided to change this. When they came to Ottawa to lobby, they met with me and asked why we could not have an area on Parliament Hill devoted to the "Famous Five." I thought it was a wonderful idea, and immediately approached the Speaker, the Honourable Gilbert Parent. Gilbert was very sympathetic but warned me that the rules of the Hill forbade anyone but a head of state or a head of government to occupy a place of prominence. Thus, the only statue of a woman on the hill was that of Queen Elizabeth, who personally unveiled a beautiful bronze of herself mounted on a horse when she came to Canada during her "annus horribilis" in 1992.

I told Gilbert that I didn't care what the convention said, and pointed out that a statue of Thomas D'Arcy McGee graced the bottom of the hill, although he was neither a monarch nor a prime minister. Gil chuckled and said he was sympathetic but powerless to do anything unless I had the consent of all parties of the House. So, I thanked him and got to work. The first part was easy. I secured the support of every political party for a resolution to empower the House of Commons to break all the rules and let the "Famous Five" be recognized on the Hill. I approached Deb Grey from the Alliance, Elsie Wayne from the Conservatives, Suzanne Tremblay from the Bloc Québécois and Alexa McDonough from the NDP. Even though we were all from different political parties, we shared a common bond of parliamentary sisterhood. Deb Grey had been alone when she came to the Hill as a Reform member, and Suzanne Tremblay, an avowed separatist, often worked closely with us on issues that were of benefit to women. Elsie Wayne, the mother hen of the Conservative Party, immediately saw the political advantage in supporting this great project. As for Alexa, she was instantly supportive. An avowed feminist, she quickly saw the symbolic importance of the Famous Five project. Within a few days, all of them had secured an agreement in principle from their respective parties to support an all-party motion in the House. Next, I had to find an appropriate MP to introduce the resolution because it was to be done under private members' business. I asked Jean Augustine, and she was thrilled to play a part in making history, not only for women, but hopefully for all Canadians.

We had a great team, led by then Deputy Whip Marlene Catterall. It is the job of the government whip to push legislation through the House and what better person to do so than the first female deputy whip in the history of Canada? We all assumed that with the support of all parties, the legislation would sail through the House and the Senate. We were so wrong. We knew that we were operating on a tight time frame because parliamentary approval was just the first step in a long process to have the Famous Five statue unveiled in time for an anniversary. The clock was ticking and we assumed the House would have no problem passing the legislation. We forgot, however, to account for the potential role of independent MP John Nunziata as a spoiler. In order for the legislation to be passed, it required *unanimous* consent and in our haste we had forgotten to ask John for his approval. To be fair to my old Rat Pack colleague, John was not against the legislation in principle; he was just annoyed, as an Independent, that he had not been consulted. As speeches from all sides of the House in support of the legislation continued, John remained glued to his seat, ready to object if any attempt was made to have the bill passed. Hours elapsed, the clock was ticking, and it seemed as though time was running out for changing the face of Parliament Hill. John didn't account for womanly wiles. Marlene Catterall kept her eye on John all day. And at one point, as we all must do sooner or later, he had to leave the Chamber to see a man about a horse. In two minutes, Marlene managed to get unanimous consent and by the time John returned to his seat he was startled to find that the legislation had moved on to the Senate for what we hoped was speedy parliamentary approval.

In the Senate we ran into Colin Kenny, a shrewd ex-aide to prime minister Trudeau. Colin had a cherubic face and an iron will; when he decided to get something done, woe betide the parliamentarian who stood in his way. Colin was thorough and engaging. It was his initiative, a private member's bill, that led to the first initiative to "green" Parliament Hill. At that time, Colin was working hard to save a green space in Ottawa's downtown core that was about to be turned into condominiums. He had approached me in my capacity as minister responsible for the National Capital Commission to stop the development. Since the NCC was a Crown corporation at arm's length from the government, I advised Colin that I could not. He then asked me to declare the site a national park. I told him if I were ever going to take the flak for designating a parking lot as a national park, it would be in my riding, not in the nation's capital. Next, to his credit, Senator Kenny came up with a brilliant idea; he would offer the site to the Famous Five statue if it were not approved for Parliament Hill. However, once parliamentary approval came from the Commons, the Senator decided he would block the bill to get what he wanted. I was in Europe on government business, and debate was about to close for the year when I received a panicky phone call from Ottawa. Senator Kenny would block the bill unless I gave him a commitment in writing that the parking lot known as the Daly site would be turned into a national park. I played a game of transatlantic chicken. I told my assistant to inform Senator Kenny in no uncertain terms that I would never submit to pressure tactics like this and we would dare him to be the parliamentarian who blocked the arrival of the "Famous Five" on the Hill. He blinked, and the Senate passed the legislation.

In the new year, we began the planning for the unveiling of the Famous Five statue two years hence. One of the key players who helped move this project along was Alphonse Gagliano. One would not necessarily have considered Alphonse a feminist, but he pushed very hard to ensure that all the planning required by his Public Works Department was speedily completed. Without his support, our initiative would never have been successful. I also had great help from friend and feminist Isabel Metcalfe. Since she lived in Ottawa, she was able to keep in touch with all the players on a regular basis to make sure the work was done. And last but not least, was my friend and fellow political traveller, Alice Willems. Alice knew how long things normally took in politics so she pushed long and hard to ensure that this statue grouping was erected in record time in 2000. To put it in context, Mr. Trudeau died that year. Following advice from the family, I approved the erection of a statue in his honour in 2002. It is scheduled to be unveiled in 2005. In retrospect, Senator Kenny and I were both on the right track. The development he was trying to block should never have happened. The Famous Five statue is now the most visited and photographed group statue on the Hill.

What does all this have to do with power? Well, in fact only one of those famous five women ever set foot in Parliament as an MP and yet each one of them did more to change the course of Canadian history than dozens of those who are honoured within the halls of Parliament. Power, in other words, does not necessarily rest in the hands of the office-holder. The fact that one is an MP or a minister or even a prime minister is not necessarily a guarantee of power. Power is much more relevant as an instrument of empowerment. Power held by an individual does not naturally increase. If it is not used, it atrophies and eventually disappears.

Some of the most important political figures of the twentieth century, both good and evil, found that their source of power did not come from a political hierarchy but rather from an idea. One man, Nelson Mandela, exercised more power from a jail cell than most political leaders do in a lifetime. He believed all people are created equal and that pluralism as a basis for a free society is the most empowering model. True power comes not from might but from an idea, and if you truly believe that all change comes from within, each person has the power to change the world.

The Famous Five showed that all power does not come only from heads of state or government. In fact, the long-term power attached to real change actually comes from the ground up, from the people. Nelson Mandela was able to pursue a dream of equality from a jail cell because that dream was supported by millions of people who could not even vote in their own country. Two millennia after his death, the power of Jesus Christ still fuels the notion that the true values of Christianity lie in what we do for our brothers and sisters. And that is why, to harness the power of humanity, we need to focus not on building bigger armies, but on promoting, and thus empowering, diversity and equality.

Empowerment

We in North America were in the lead of women's empowerment in the twentieth century. We changed our laws and opened the doors to true equality. But the structures that reflect our changed reality have yet to change. In the twenty-first century, women still have to fight to have their place on the Hill, literally and figuratively. Just seven years after throwing off the yoke of apartheid, Nelson Mandela's South Africa has more women in Parliament than Canada has had in our country's entire 137 years.

It is no accident that fewer women and minorities choose politics as their vehicles for empowerment. Similarly, in the financial and media sectors, the number of women and minorities in the upper management echelons is laughably small. When it comes to government, we actually have more women and minorities in cabinet than we do in the public service. I remember seeing my first black public servant in the cabinet room some ten years after I became a minister.

This lack of empowerment was highlighted at the 2003 Press Gallery dinner. It is always a high-level affair representing a who's who of the Canadian political and media elite. This year it was a sellout crowd as hundreds of journalists, politicos, and flacks crowded the room to see the send-off for Prime Minister Chrétien and the debut of Jack Layton, Peter Mackay, and Stephen Harper. It was a chance to judge and be judged, a chance for the new leaders to strut their stuff before a well-lubricated and cynical "seen it all before" gallery. It was an evening where careers would be made or broken. In fact, so important is the buzz from the gallery dinner that Bloc Québécois leader Gilles Duceppe, notorious for his barbed wit aimed at others and his own thin skin, even issued press releases to announce why he would no longer be attending press gallery dinners (after a couple of attempts at wit so feeble he became the victim of bun attack). Such a night can resonate for months by humanizing or by burying leaders forever, and it also provided the invited guests with a chance to get their message out.

My first invitation to a dinner was in 1982. Politicians cannot invite themselves – they must be invited by journalists – and that year, I received an invitation from *Toronto Star* journalist David Vienneau. Over the years, I have heard some great speeches. At one point, all speeches were off the record, so you really had a chance to see a leader uncut. In recent years, it has actually been carried live on television so the humour is considerably cleaner. Among the funniest performances ever were those staged by two governors general, Jeanne Sauvé and Adrienne Clarkson. Sauvé had a reputation for being stiff. She made sure to dispel that impression with a brilliant speech. She walked into the room escorted by a footman holding the governor general's seal, and immediately started joking about her seal, using the French translation for a baby seal, "phoque." The play on words was hilarious and the ice was broken. Adrienne Clarkson used a similar brilliant stroke in her first appearance before the Press Gallery. In her public appearances she always wore avant-garde creations from Canadian designers and was taking a little flak in the press for looking dowdy. So she actually showed up at the dinner wearing a housecoat and giant pouffy slippers. It was hilarious. She immediately showed she had a sense of humour and, more importantly, could laugh at herself.

On this important night in 2003, with so much riding on the outcome for Stephen Harper, Jack Layton, and even the absent Paul Martin, I surveyed the audience, looking to see who truly defined the message in the nation's capital. I found that I could count the number of non-Caucasians on one hand. As for women, we were there in good numbers. Even the press gallery executive had good gender balance, for once. But when I looked around to see the faces that most Canadians would know, I saw mostly one ethnicity and one gender reflected. Craig Oliver, Peter Mansbridge, Don Newman, Stéphane Bureau, and so on.

It is amazing that now all these years since Barbara Frum's death and Pamela Wallin's untimely broadcasting demise, TV networks in Canada can't point to a woman anchor. Why is it that the "most trusted voice in Canadian news" is never a woman? If a woman has longevity in a new role, it is usually in the local or weekend slot. What is even more challenging is that most media and political types would argue that, sure, equality exists. We (women, minorities, etc.) "just haven't taken advantage of the opportunities." So is it any wonder that one of the most poignant TV clips on the first night of voting in the so-called Liberal leadership race in 2003 was an elderly woman from Nova Scotia sporting a Paul Martin button who stated plaintively that "Canada is not ready for a woman prime minister."

Is it any wonder that the greatest number of successful businesses in the last decade have been started by women and minorities? Set free from the glass ceilings of the political and financial world, they soar. Oversimplification? Just ask yourself why in seven short years the Republic of South Africa was able to exceed Canada in the empowerment of women and minorities. If we don't even acknowledge the problem, if we continue to bask in our own unrealistic description as a totally open, egalitarian society, if we continue to ignore the warning bells on the status of women here published by the United Nations Human Development Index, we will continue to fall further behind. We are thirty-sixth in the world in women's involvement in politics.

By contrast we face our geographic challenges with gusto. We reflect constantly on the dissonance between the East and the West and the economic challenges facing Atlantic Canadians. We even assume that constitutional amendments will heal the wounds that fester constantly between Quebec and the rest of Canada. But seldom and certainly not in mainstream political discourse do we acknowledge that five decades after women were given equality in the law and equal pay legislation was tabled in Parliament, the year I was born, we still do not have equality in law and in pay. Worse, if we intend to be successful competing in a man's world, we dare not even complain about it.

When she retired from politics Judy LaMarsh wrote an auto-biography – *A Bird in a Gilded Cage* – in which she recalled the struggles she faced in surviving in a man's world. I don't want my daughter to be writing the same kind of book thirty years from now.

As a young woman growing up in politics, I remember looking for role models. I remember how proud I was to see the work of the Honourable Monique Bégin in building the debate toward the Canada Health Act more than twenty years ago. I remember the Honourable Judy Erola leading the charge to ensure that women were given true equality in the Constitution Act, 1982. It may be hard to believe now, but in the heat of the debate to repatriate the Canadian Constitution, it was decided that a "notwithstanding" clause would be introduced to ensure that certain rights were not bestowed without some limitations. Since some provincial premiers had concerns about the legal ramifications of the Charter of Rights and Freedoms, it was agreed that an overarching "escape" clause, known as the "notwithstanding" clause would be added to the changes to ensure provincial support.

In repatriating the Constitution from the mother Parliament in England, it seemed that Canadian women's equality would be forever subject to this "notwithstanding" clause. Women across the country were horrified that years after our equality had been enshrined in the law, if not in life, it was to be bargained away by eleven men. We sprang into action.

I was a provincial MPP at the time and worked in a non-partisan way with the other women in the legislature (all six of us) to put pressure on all governments, federal and provincial, to exclude women from the despised clause. Our efforts were successful. April 17 remains an important day on the political calendar for women's equality for Canada, the day when women's rights were not traded away in the constant federal-provincial bickering that characterizes so much of Canadian politics.

If you go back and review the great constitutional debates from those days that form such an important framework for the Canadian political identity, it is as though the struggle for women's equality didn't exist; as though the only thing that really mattered in the Canadian Constitution was the division of power between the Canadian government and the provinces; as though the definition of the federation was more important than the lives of those who lived in it.

Never was the trump card of constitutionalism played with more disregard for the people than in the Meech Lake debate. Never was there a more misunderstood document or a more fragile time for Canada. And in the middle of it all, as in the middle of most of the great Canadian debates, was a cleavage in the Liberal Party of Canada that reflected the cleavage in the country.

Chapter Three

The Dice Rolls and the Country Loses

As a newly minted member of Parliament in 1984, I basked in the reflected historic glory of working within the Centre Block of the Parliament buildings. But perhaps as fascinating was the opportunity to work in Canada's two official languages. As a lover of languages, I had studied three at university and had received an Honours degree in French and English. The prospect of working in bilingual Ottawa was like a dream come true. What an opportunity to put the principles of duality and diversity into action! Or so I thought. Little did I realize that the historic differences between the so-called two founding nations were not only nurtured on Parliament Hill, they would, from time to time, become enflamed by the very people whose stated goal was bringing the country together. Such was the sorry saga of the Meech Lake debate.

Prime Minister Brian Mulroney came to power in the September 4 massacre that saw the Liberal majority of almost two decades reduced to a shell-shocked band of forty members.

Mulroney had grown up in the heart of Quebec, and like many an Irishman, he had developed a special bond with French Canadians. He talked like them, he worked like them, and he even knew how to have fun like them. While the rest of Canada sometimes reviled Mr. Mulroney, Quebecers liked him and even felt he was one of theirs. In fact, in history a common mistrust of the English often united French Canadians and their Irish neighbours. It is said that up to 40 per cent of unilingual French Quebecers today have some Irish blood coursing through their veins.

I remember the first year I attended the Press Gallery dinner with David Vienneau, which spilled over into the press building. In those days, the party went on all night, and liquor laws didn't apply in the parliamentary precinct. At about four a.m., Brian Mulroney, a fine baritone, gathered around the piano with journalist Mike Duffy to sing "When Irish Eyes Are Smiling." Brian Mulroney was very proud of his Irish roots, making sure to remind all those of similar heritage (including the Copps family) that we shared a common bond. He sang the same song on stage with Ronald Reagan at the Summit in Quebec. Duff was also a proud Irishman, although his family had detoured to Prince Edward Island where even today his mother (a lady in her eighties) nightly critiques his CTV show. Mulroney went so far as to tie John Nunziata into the Irish connection when he invited John and his Irish-born wife, Caroline, to join him on a government trip to Ireland.

Brian Mulroney certainly had the gift of Irish blarney but he also had a way of genuinely making people feel at home, and so it only made sense that his first and defining political objective was to ensure that Quebecers became part of the Canadian constitutional family. In 1982, when the Constitution was repatriated, the Quebec government of the day refused to sign. If you talk to separatists, they'll tell you that the refusal was tied to the so-called Night of the Long Knives, the night when federal ministers (including Jean Chrétien) got together with the other premiers to cut a secret deal on the amending formula. Quebec's separatist premier René Lévesque, outsmarted and isolated by Pierre Trudeau, characterized the deal as a betrayal and summarily left the First Ministers Conference.

When Mr. Mulroney came to office he had managed to do what no Conservative before him had done. His carefully crafted coalition of chagrined Westerners and soft Quebec nationalists was so successful that he brought the largest majority of any Parliament into office in 1984. And one of his commitments, bringing Quebec into the Canadian family, involved a cast of characters whose impact on Canadian politics would be felt for many years to come. He invited his friend Lucien Bouchard, a successful and charismatic lawyer, to sign on to federalism and Conservatism at the same time. He elevated a young superstar from Sherbrooke to ministerial status and Jean Charest went on to play a role in two political parties at both the federal and provincial levels of government. In the early days, Charest had to resign from his junior minister's position, yet Mulroney entrusted him with brokering a compromise when it looked as though his beloved Meech Lake was in trouble. Yet from his days as a labour lawyer and businessman Mulroney was used to taking a deal close to the brink, and relished the one-upmanship of clinching the deal. There were five conditions to Meech Lake.

1. The right for Quebec to appoint three judges to the Supreme Court of Canada in perpetuity. (Since Quebec was the only province operating under a different, civil law, this did not seem unreasonable.)

2. Recognition of Quebec as a distinct society. (Having worked in Quebec as a journalist myself, I thought this one would be a no-brainer, because it reflected reality, linguistically and culturally.)

3. Minimum representation in Parliament. (Since Prince Edward Island with a current population of 130,000 received a similar constitutional guarantee of four seats, it seemed that there was a reasonable precedent for this.)

4. Setting out specific provincial powers for immigration (enshrining in the Constitution a practice that had already been adopted in the Cullen-Couture agreement on immigration and settlement) and requiring financial compensation for opting out of federal programs, to spend in areas of exclusive provincial jurisdiction.

5. A process for specific Senate reform and an interim requirement that future Senators shall be chosen by the Government of Canada from a list provided by provincial governments.

All in all, the amendments seemed reasonable to me, a novice with an abiding love for the French language and a keen desire to see the government support the survival and growth of the distinct nature of Quebec and recognize the unique contribution of French Canada to the identity of the country.

Liberal Leader John Turner agreed. Guided by his Quebec lieutenant Raymond Garneau and the wily André Ouellet, Turner was of the view that the Meech Lake Accord was a reasonable price to pay for peace in the Canadian family. He urged his forty-member caucus to follow him in support of the Accord. In fact, Mulroney, in an attempt to secure unanimity, had required not only the Parliament of Canada but also each provincial legislative assembly to vote on the package, and he provided three years for the process to be completed.

In retrospect, the long time frame from start to finish was probably the death of Meech. Any student of government will tell you that controversial measures, once decided upon, should be dealt with swiftly, because those who are opposed, however small in number, will continue to organize, while those who are in favour will agree and move on to other issues.

For example, our own government's new law on gun control demonstrated the danger in delay. When the legislation was first introduced, it was supported by more than 80 per cent of Canadians. A year later, the legislation still had not been ratified, and the public debate saw support plummet by 30 per cent. In the end, although the majority still supported the legislation, they had moved on to worry about other issues while the vocal opponents of the legislation continued to gather steam, and public support. And so it was with Meech.

As the Prime Minister and the House of Commons prepared to vote, debate swirled across the country. Aboriginal people were opposed because in this major constitutional amendment (perhaps the last to be seen in a generation) their issues had not even been mentioned. Westerners, anxious for a Triple-E senate, saw Meech as just another stalling tactic, delaying Senate reform. Even Liberals, especially those who pursued Mr. Trudeau's vision of a bilingual, multicultural Canada where each Canadian had the right and even the responsibility to pursue a linguistic duality that did not respect provincial borders, saw this as the end to their dream of a country where all Canadians pursued diversity.

As a pragmatist, I did not share their concerns. I believed that the French-speaking people of Quebec had every reason to feel threatened, sandwiched as they were in the middle of a North American continent of more than 320 million anglophones. As an anglophone who loved the French language and culture enough to learn to speak it fluently and defend it passionately, I remember how hard it was to maintain my French while I worked as an MPP at Queen's Park. I had personally seen on many occasions how even the government of Canada ignored the requirement to operate in both official languages in many parts of the country. So while I sympathized with the dream of one united bilingual Canada, I feared the reality was leading us toward one united monocultural North America. Anything the Canadian Constitution could do to protect the "distinctiveness of the French language" was worth doing.

In my own party Mr. Turner was able to convince the majority of members of Parliament that the Meech Lake agreement was worth supporting. The members who opposed the accord had some high-powered support, especially in the person of the former prime minister and avowed federalist, the Right Honourable Pierre Elliott Trudeau.

The Free Trade Wars

The election of 1988 started out with a whimper. The polls were predicting disaster for the Liberals and a day didn't seem to go by without another nail being pounded into John Turner's coffin. The Party brass were working furiously on a plan to replace Mr. Turner right in the middle of the campaign, based on the premise that he could not win – and in the Liberal family, winning was what mattered. As we were slugging it out door to door, trying to convince voters to come on side, our own party seemed determined to self-destruct. A tell-all insider's tale called *Reign of Error*, a book by Greg Westin which portrayed a leader's office in disarray, a visionless chief, and a party going into a tailspin provided the backdrop for a dispirited campaign. At one point, we awoke to newspaper head-lines suggesting that a group of key Liberals, led by the doyen of the party, the Honourable Herb Gray, had gone to John Turner to convince him that the only hope for Liberal survival was for him to step down and pave the way for Jean Chrétien to take over. Of course, when the news broke, all and sundry denied up and down that anything of the sort had taken place. We were in damage control, big time, and the polls showed the best we could hope for was to stay ahead of the third place New Democrats to remain the Official Opposition.

And then came the TV debate. In the 1984 campaign, the knockout punch had been delivered by Brian Mulroney when he accused John Turner of gross patronage abuses, to which Turner lamely replied "I had no option." Mulroney hit Turner between the eyes, "You had an option, sir," and that exchange forever crys-tallized John Turner's image as a leader weakened by decisions made for him, not by him. Mulroney went on to sweep Liberals out from almost every nook and cranny in the country. In 1988, it was John Turner's chance to deliver the knockout blow. And this time, it was not about style, it was about substance: whether or not to pursue the Free Trade Agreement that Mr. Mulroney had put in the window as the economic salvation of Canada.

Once again the Liberal Party seemed split along linguistic lines. Most Quebecers, proud of the success of Quebec Inc., and open to the world thanks to their new emphasis on small business, were in favour of the agreement. Most Liberals outside Quebec were not part of the business class and spurned the notion that greater inte-gration with the United States would bring prosperity and harmony to Canada. Turner seemed caught right in the middle. A

Bay Street lawyer, he seemed a natural to pursue the free trade agenda so embraced by the Business Council on National Issues. And yet, in the course of the campaign, his arguments against signing the agreement became more pointed and cogent. In fact on the evening of the great debate, when he boldly suggested that the future of Canada would be sold out by signing the agreement, his voice resonated with the people. In the wake of the debate, we immediately saw our numbers climb and the admen promptly did their magic. The next ad showed a Canada–U.S. border being erased by the signing of the agreement. John Turner's concern resonated with the population and set the stage for an election result that saw us more than double the number of Liberal MPs in the House of Commons. So his strong debate performance had snatched not victory, but survival from the jaws of Liberal annihilation. It set the stage for another showdown, one that would finally give Jean Chrétien the leadership.

Notwithstanding the surprising rise in Liberal numbers in the dying days of the campaign, it became obvious that John Turner would never lead the Liberal Party to victory. He announced his desire to step down, and the campaign to replace him began in earnest. We already knew that Jean Chrétien, who ran "first in our hearts" (in Iona Campagnolo's words) in the last campaign, would be a candidate. We also knew that Paul Martin had been touted in the media as a possible future leader as early as 1985 and his team was already building toward an all-out effort.

While the campaign unfolded, so did plans for the leadership convention. Unfortunately the brains trust in the Liberal Party agreed to have the convention on the very weekend of the potential ratification or death of the Meech Lake Accord, a date which also coincided with the celebration of St. Jean Baptiste Day. St. Jean

Baptiste had been named the patron saint of French Canadians. But over time the day had come to symbolize the celebration of Quebec's potential separation from Canada, so the decision to hold the vote on the Accord, *and* the Liberal Leadership Convention *and* St. Jean Baptiste Day in the same week was potent symbolism indeed. In fact, Paul Martin, whose support for the Accord would be positively contrasted in Quebec with his rival Jean Chrétien's opposition, saw it as a potential coup.

The support for Meech in Quebec, however, was balanced by bitter opposition in Atlantic Canada and the West. Atlantic-Canadian opposition galvanized around Premier Clyde Wells of Newfoundland, whose vast island province with four hundred years of history (and, some would say, its own language) could also rightly lay claim to being a distinct society. Moving westward, staunch Chrétien loyalist and leader of the Liberal Party of Manitoba, Sharon Carstairs, was an articulate opponent of the agreement and eventually managed to develop a consensus of opposition in Manitoba, which included the now famous opposition of MLA Elijah Harper. His lone eagle feather of protest ensured that the Manitoba Legislature did not vote on the Accord. While Manitoba was avoiding a vote and Newfoundland had not yet made a decision, the clock on the Liberal leadership race was ticking.

In fact, history will show that the most damaging blow to the Accord came in an interview granted by Prime Minister Brian Mulroney to Susan Delacourt and Graham Fraser of the *Globe and Mail* some months before. In the course of the interview Mr. Mulroney broke the basic rule of collective bargaining – don't speak until the agreement is signed. Mulroney was a practical political fixer. In his previous life's work as a labour lawyer, he had a wonderful reputation for toughness and success. He had one political liability, which was also his greatest gift. Like most politicians, he liked to talk. And when it came to deal-making, he wanted to underline his role in the deal. This time, he talked too much before the deal was done. In a very candid interview, Mulroney said he treated the Accord's negotiation like any labour negotiation. He brought the premiers together, created a deliberate sense of crisis and pushed them to the brink, in the belief they would sign the agreement. "I rolled the dice," he bragged, and they all blinked, as he thought they would. The only problem was that the interview pre-dated the ratification required by every legislature, and even though the premiers had promised to put the issue to their legislatures, they hadn't promised to ratify it. So in the hours leading up to the leadership convention, two legislatures, Newfoundland's and Manitoba's, had not yet voted.

As a dark-horse candidate I entered the leadership race in late January. Looking back on it, I have to wonder if my enthusiasm for all things political overcame my good sense. Realistically, I didn't stand a chance. My "national" campaign team did not even have co-chairs in every province on the day before we were to launch the campaign. To fill a gap in Nova Scotia, I actually had to convince Tory Marie Hodgson to join the Liberal Party and then become my campaign chair in Nova Scotia, all in the same day. Marie, the aunt of Bob Speller, who went on to become Agriculture Minister was the only person in Nova Scotia we could convince to jump aboard our team. Yet for all our inexperience, we ran a campaign that managed to elect delegates from across the country and on a shoestring budget we managed to secure 499 votes, a little less than half of the votes secured by Paul Martin. Our combined effort was not enough to even nip at Chrétien's heels but that didn't mean the leadership weekend would pass without notice in the Liberal Party. In fact, the final vote was held in the Saddledome and the buzz of the convention was the decision about whether Meech would live or die.

In the meantime, Mr. Mulroney had worked hard to hang the responsibility for the death of Meech (if it happened that way) on the shoulders of Jean Chrétien, as he rightly surmised that Mr. Chrétien might be the next leader of the Liberal Party of Canada. As the temperature on the issue rose in Quebec, so the ardour in Ontario for a deal diminished, and members of Mulroney's own party and Canadians in general began to get cold feet about the Accord. In the leadup to the convention, and in the fallout of his "roll the dice" comments, Mulroney had to put some water in his wine to address some of the concerns being raised, even by those who had originally voted in favour of the Accord. To that end, he named young, charismatic Jean Charest to work on proposals to meet the concerns expressed by various opponents across the country. But as Jean Charest worked to achieve a consensus, Lucien Bouchard, a long-time nationalist who had answered Brian Mulroney's call to federalism, made it clear that he would not compromise. While Liberals moved toward the leadership convention, Mr. Bouchard announced that he could not support the Charest proposals and that his betrayal by the Prime Minister left him no choice but to leave the Conservative Party. And so the Bloc Québécois was born. Within a few days the fledgling party would be joined by the co-chair of Paul Martin's unsuccessful leadership campaign, Jean Lapierre.

As we prepared our speeches going into the convention, we had no idea whether Meech would live or die. In fact, the Newfoundland House of Assembly was voting on the Accord during the beginning of the convention, and convention co-chairs had to extend registration especially for Clyde Wells so that he could attend the Liberal leadership convention after having cast his ballot against Meech. He was greeted with howls of outrage from Quebec delegates for his rejection of Meech, particularly since he had been with all the premiers when the original proposal had been put forward three years earlier. Wells's answer? He had only promised to bring the issue to the Assembly, not to vote in favour of it. Meanwhile, his strong support for Jean Chrétien created a convention dilemma, given the emotional climate of the Meech debate. When the Newfoundland vote killed the Accord, Clyde Wells got to the convention just in time to embrace his long-time friend and political ally Jean Chrétien. They say one picture is worth a thousand words. In this case, their public embrace was seen as a total betrayal by those Quebecers who had supported the Accord, among them Jean Lapierre and Paul Martin.

That was a key moment in the division which would continue to fester in the Liberal Party. Somehow the bitterness at losing the Meech Lake fight became mixed with the bitterness at losing the leadership. Jean Lapierre and David Herle and a number of other Martin supporters began the first night under Mr. Chrétien's leadership wearing black armbands and shrieking "*vendu*," "sellout," and "traitor" at him in the convention, while other Liberals looked on in horror.

It was part of a Martin team pattern noted by John Gray in his book. Of David Herle, he wrote "his reputation is that he takes no prisoners. In 1990, when it was clear that Martin had no chance of beating Chrétien, Herle was one of those who kept pushing for every last vote and every last elbow in the ribs, whether or not the ribs belonged to a fellow Liberal, because, in politics as in those games you play only to win, there are no Marquis of Queensberry rules."

Very shortly thereafter, Jean Lapierre left the Liberal Party and joined Lucien Bouchard, along with fellow Liberal MP Gilles Rocheleau. The pair became founding members of the Bloc and helped pave the way for the referendum that very nearly lost Canada. Meanwhile, the animosity against Jean Chrétien, our new leader, mounted in Quebec. Just as he was loved by Anglo-Canadians who embraced his folksy manner and "little guy from Shawinigan" directness, he was despised in equal measure by many of the political elites in Quebec who blamed him for the "betrayal" they perceived in the defeat of Meech. So polarized had the debate become that Quebecers who had never read a word of the Constitution were absolutely convinced that their continued adherence to Canada was dependent on this document that they had never read. The Liberals who left the Party the day Mr. Chrétien was elected joined with those who had abandoned the Conservatives and piled up the fuel for a political firestorm that would consume Canada.

Chapter Four

Jean Chrétien Takes Charge

The night that Jean Lapierre, David Herle, Terrie O'Leary, and other members of the failed Martin bid were sporting their armbands and yelling abuse at Jean Chrétien, my small band of 499 supporters immediately joined in behind the new Leader to begin the work of getting back to government. The morning after the vote, the new Leader had called an early caucus meeting to lay out a simple road map for restoring people's faith in the Liberal Party and ultimately in Canada. Bleary-eyed members showed up for the first caucus meeting under the leadership of Jean Chrétien as he established a pattern that was to serve him well in government. The meeting started on time. And he gave each caucus member a chance to be heard. He knew emotions were running high after the leadership fight and had some sage advice to let emotions calm down over the summer: get out, travel, and get to know your country. Of course the media sneered at the message, accusing the Leader of being trite at a time when the country was fracturing.

But Jean Chrétien knew Canada a little better than they did. He knew that by and large Canadians were suffering from serious constitutional fatigue and the best way to build a country was not through political deals but through Canadians getting to know each other.

That, however, was easier said than done. With a country encompassing six time zones, speaking two official languages and dozens of other tongues, the greatest challenge for Canada was not finding a constitutional agreement but a feeling of attachment. When Jean Chrétien spoke about his attachment to Canada, he wore his heart on his sleeve. He was a small-town francophone who had come to the nation's capital without knowing a word of English and yet grew to be loved by anglophones across the country. Despite his strong accent and jumbled syntax, his sense of attachment to the natural wonder of Canada came through loud and clear. He often spoke with pride about how, in his role as minister responsible for Indian and Northern Affairs and minister responsible for Parks, he once established a park in Baffin Island. He was overflying a remote area with his devoted partner, Aline, and they saw a natural site so beautiful that he turned to his wife and said he was going to designate it a national park in her honour. He told Aline he had to consult first with the Minister for Indian Affairs (himself), and the Minister for Northern Development (himself again), and the Minister for Parks. Since they all agreed, at that moment he was able to establish a national park, which remains today one of the natural jewels in the Canadian Parks Agency.

His love for Parks was a great asset to me when I moved to pass a controversial new law ending all development in Canada's national parks. When we received a report from Unesco that Banff was at risk of losing World Heritage status because of environmental degradation, something had to be done. I moved quickly with a law that capped park development and ensured that any capital construction projects in the parks had to have no environmental impact. I was ridiculed in the Calgary media but surveys showed that the vast majority of Canadians, especially Albertans, supported the moves. I had to fight considerable pressure from the development community and it was the Prime Minister's support that paved the way for legislation that was supported by all parties in the House, including the Reform Party. Their critic, Jim Abbott, lived in the Rocky Mountains area himself and had a great understanding of the vital importance of the natural state of the Rockies; his work was crucial in securing all-party approval.

One of the lessons Chrétien had drawn from the almost three decades he spent in Parliament before he became prime minister was that the diversity of Canada – in both geography and demography – was a unique feature of our country which should be cherished and celebrated. Years later, I remember attending the Banff Television Festival in that idyllic setting in the Rockies. I was stopped in the hallway by a young Quebec cinematographer who had never travelled in the West. She spoke only French and exclaimed breathlessly to me that she had never seen any place as beautiful as the Rocky Mountains and now she finally understood why it would be folly to split this country apart. Chrétien had understood that truth for a long time, even speaking proudly to Quebecers about "our Rockies." He tried to get us all to understand it that morning at the caucus meeting when he emphasized why "we have much work to do," and that the principles of hard work and opening ourselves to see other parts of the country would be great summer preparation for the long road ahead to government.

Politics and Family

There is probably no other job in Canada that permits you, as part of your job description, to get to know your country. There is probably no other country with the cultural, linguistic, and geographic diversity we have inherited, and the opportunity to visit every nook and cranny builds the kind of knowledge and love of Canada that very few people can share. But with distance also come family challenges.

Danelle's dad and I split up when she was less than three years old. Like any divorce, it was painful for Ric and me, but Danelle was too young to remember the hardship. Over the years, she has maintained a good relationship with her dad, who agreed early on that I should have custody and he would visit as often as he could. During that time, she knew that she had her mom's full attention and later would make it clear that she did not want any man to come between us. The challenge of blending two families was still in the future.

By the time the leadership race was won, I was a single mom with a three-year-old daughter who had probably seen more of Canada than most adults. I had made the decision very early on that I did not want to be an absentee mother, so my daughter travelled everywhere with me until she started school, and she had friends on both coasts before she ever went to preschool. In fact, she was so used to plane travel that she would beg me to take her to work on the bus, because that was a mode of travel she was less familiar with and it was exciting, even exotic. Because politics was such a part of my life, she rapidly became used to the punishing travel schedules of her mom and thought nothing of flying out with me to Newfoundland or British Columbia while I worked on a political campaign.

One of her earliest campaign photos was taken when she was only four or five months old. I was working for Beth Phinney, who was running in a by-election on Hamilton Mountain, Danelle was a few months old, and the photographer caught her nestled in a blanket on the floor of the campaign room while Carmen Rizzotto was reviewing the canvassing strategy. When she needed a drink, I would breast-feed. Simple. Always warm, clean, and available. By the time Danelle had finished the leadership campaign she was an old pro. At three she could work a room like me and would think nothing of mimicking my speech-making the way other kids would play house.

Chrétien had the right idea about politics when he said the most important thing was for people to know each other. To this day, seventeen years later, lots of women come up and ask about my daughter because they remember the day she was born, the fact that I breast-fed her at the office, the fact that my struggles represented their struggles and my victories represented their victories. The birth and raising of Danelle spoke volumes to them about their own lives. The fact that I would dare to seek the leadership of my party gave them hope to pursue their dreams. And seventeen years later, our lives intertwine with stories of trying to meet the challenges of the teenage years. That personal contact meant so much more than any political agenda.

Danelle also enjoyed unique opportunities. When the Queen came to Parliament in 1992 to unveil her statue, the Leader asked if I would receive her. I was happy to do so, and brought Danelle along as my escort. She was instructed on how to curtsy to the Queen but, oh, how she howled about having to wear a hat. Nature looked after that problem for her by providing a particularly windy day. As we arrived on Parliament Hill the morning of the Queen's visit, Danelle's hat flew off her head and right under the wheels of a passing car. Covered with tire prints, the hat had to be sidelined, but that didn't dampen her enthusiasm for a once in a lifetime experience.

Being the child of a politician is not, however, all peaches and cream. The truth is, for every one of those great experiences, there are dozens of times when Mom is very far away, and even a phone line won't bridge the distance. I remember one especially painful memory. We were right in the middle of an effort to save the son of Meech, the Charlottetown Accord. The Accord was the result of a broader consensus that attempted to bridge the constitutional gaps in the 1982 Constitution Act. Once again, the political elites thought all the bases were covered and we even had most of the political parties on side. But the people were suspicious and the approach we all took to try to convince the electorate was to organize town halls and radio call-in appearances across the country promoting the benefits of the Accord.

I was on one such phone-in on the Bill Good show on CKNW in British Columbia pleading the benefits of Charlottetown when a particularly vicious caller phoned in. He prefaced his remarks by suggesting I should crawl back into the Eastern garbage dump that I had crawled out of and then accused me of being nothing more than a Brian Mulroney toady (which would have amused my old opponent, Mr. Mulroney, a great deal). At that point, my daughter was home with a case of head lice and chicken pox and we had recently received a kitten, which passed along a ringworm. The head lice were a school import, and the chicken pox fescues were almost impossible to separate from the lice and the ringworm. So I had one sick daughter thousands of miles away and I happened to be suffering from a bad cold myself. It was a bad time to call me garbage and a toady. I turned on the caller, suggesting that I had no reason to be away from my daughter in these circumstances but I was there, taking abuse from a caller like him, because I cared about my country. In retrospect, the Accord failed, I swayed few people on that radio show – and my daughter probably needed me more than the Bill Good show did.

That kind of dual responsibility tugs at the heartstrings of women when they pursue the dual tracks of parenthood and career. If most women in politics were granted a wish for one thing to make their job easier, it would be a wife. That is not to say that partners are not supportive. I have been married for ten years to someone who has been an incredible support in everything I do. But there is a heavy dose of guilt involved with the thousands of hours spent away from home and family to pursue the good of the country. Nonetheless, during the time when Danelle and I travelled solo, we had a chance to develop a very unique mother-daughter bond. So much so that the first time my future husband met Danelle, she was six, and he was forty-five. We had decided to go for Chinese food with his middle daughter, Sue, and Danelle as a little icebreaker. So while Sue and I went to the ladies' room, Danelle, sporting a toothy gap in her smile, turned to Austin and looked him straight in the eye to state: "You can kiss my mother but you can't marry her." Clearly one advantage of being raised in a political household is that you are ready at an early age to speak your mind.

Danelle was also present at unique moments in Canadian history but with a perspective vastly different from most political types. She was born on March 26. Upon hearing the news of her arrival, John Turner rose in the House to announce her birth. In a fatherly way, he even joked that I had timed the birth to get top billing at Question Period since she had been born only a few minutes earlier. In any case Danelle's birth made front-page news in every newspaper in the country. The broadcasting union on Parliament Hill even made a special presentation video, which highlighted the statement in the House and the early television footage of Canada's first parliamentary baby cradled in the arms of her parents hours after she became the first child born to a woman MP in the history of Canada's Parliament. It's hard to believe that happened only seventeen years ago.

Only a few days after her birth, United States President Ronald Reagan was coming to Parliament. I wanted to be there for the speech and had taken my daughter to the Hill office where she was sleeping in a little bassinet. Mr. Reagan's speech went a little longer than expected and my breasts were engorged with milk. In great discomfort I bounded to my fourth-floor office where Danelle was howling for milk. Suffice to say, I quickly learned the benefits of a breast pump to supplement mother's milk. No caregiver, however professional, can silence the cry of a hungry infant when she is far more interested in eating than in hearing a political speech, even from a visiting president.

Pay Equity

One of the first challenges facing the new government in 1993 was whether to live up to our promise on pay equity. Ironically, the women's caucus was almost unanimous on the need to move forward quickly on pay equity – equal pay for women doing the same work as men, not a hard concept to grasp. The only dissenting voices at the caucus meeting were Anne McLellan, then Justice Minister, and her friends Mary Clancy and Shaughnessy Cohen. Shaughnessy spoke out at the caucus meeting, counselling us to move slowly, given the fragile financial state of the government, a message that Anne echoed in cabinet. The Finance Minister, Paul Martin, and the Treasury Board president, Marcel Masse, both vigorously opposed a settlement. In fact the Treasury Board predicted that the settlement alone could cost the government in excess of $2 billion. Most of the Liberal women worked hard and spoke out strongly in favour of the settlement, both in caucus and in cabinet. Yet when the decision was made not to go ahead, the newspaper headlines attacked me and other women in the caucus for being so weak that we were unable to get the payment through – with not a word about the role of the Minister of Finance and the Treasury Board president who literally held the keys to the equity kingdom.

We women in caucus never stopped working for pay equity and when Lucienne Robillard replaced Marcel Masse as the president of the Treasury Board, the Board's predictions on the cost of settlement mysteriously dropped drastically, and within a few months the settlement had been reached. Once pay equity became the law, however, the same journalists who had trashed the women in the caucus for our ineffectiveness had little to say about how soon after Lucienne Robillard moved into Treasury Board, the problem was very effectively solved. *Deux poids, deux mesures.* A double standard, best described and understood in French.

Finding Love

During the period when I was aggressively recruiting women candidates, I also managed to keep in touch with any potential candidates in many parts of the country. One such potential candidate (I thought) was Austin Thorne, the secretary-treasurer of the Canadian Federation of Labour who developed the first venture capital fund for workers outside the province of Quebec. I met

Austin early in my time in Ottawa when, as labour critic for the Liberals in the mid-eighties, it was my job to keep in touch with unions and scout out the latest trends in union–government dialogue that might help form the basis for our future platform. In the early nineties, when Austin left the labour movement, I thought he would make a great Liberal candidate to run against my old sparring partner John Crosbie in his hometown of St. John's, Newfoundland. In fact, our first choice was Roseanne Cashin, the ex-wife of Richard Cashin and a formidable political force in her own right. I suspected, however, that Roseanne was getting cold feet (who wouldn't, running against John Crosbie?) Besides, it never hurts to have a fallback position in politics so I wanted him to come to my office one morning. I didn't realize, of course, that John Crosbie would decide not to enter the election of 1993, and neither did Austin. At our meeting over coffee he told me frankly that he thought John Crosbie was unbeatable, making it clear that he would not be part of our campaign. Little did I know that Austin would soon begin another kind of campaign, a campaign for my heart.

In the summer of 1993 we began a romance that would lead to marriage the next year. And in that marriage I found a soulmate whose support and understanding made me wonder how I had ever survived on my own, both before my first marriage and after it broke up. To this day, I marvel at those moms and dads who raise families without the soft shoulder of a partner to cry on from time to time. Even as a couple, it is not easy to survive the rough-and-tumble world of politics, but solo it can be a very lonely, almost impossibly hard, road.

After working and travelling in the labour movement for so many years and knowing the lonely rigours of constant travel away from home, Austin provided the wisdom of experience and a port in the storm. The comparison is a good one, because Austin's father was a fisherman, and his earliest memories were of weathering the storms off the Grand Banks in a seventeen-foot dory as a young child. So no political storm could swallow him up. Besides this calm support, he brought three beautiful children to our marriage. Blended marriages are everywhere in the modern world, but nothing prepares you for the challenges involved in bringing not just two people, but two families and their different cultures together. It was hard work, but so fruitful.

We took all our children on our honeymoon in 1994. Three weeks together on a charter in the British Virgin Islands proved to be a great bonding experience. Austin was captain, I was first mate, and the kids were crew. We not only enjoyed the best vacation ever; we are planning a tenth anniversary trip this year to celebrate it with children and grandchildren. So my time in government coincided with a new, rich chapter in my personal life. I honestly don't know if I could have survived the challenges of government – the pressure, the stress, the scrutiny, the criticism – on my own.

Without a doubt some of the toughest hours of pain in politics are inflicted as much on members of the family as they are on the politician. I know that some of the worst moments in my political life had to do with hurtful untruths written about me that had nothing to do with public policy and everything to do with portraying me as an unfeeling bitch who would even lock her poor dog in the car, or toss a handicapped person from a plane, or have what was supposedly her vagina paraded all over *Hustler* magazine. When untruths were written about me, I sued, and got retractions. But the deep hurt felt by my family members took more than a lawsuit to heal: you can imagine how my mother and my daughter felt about *Hustler* targeting me in that way because its owners disliked the new magazine law we passed in Parliament.

Some irresponsible reporters seem to think that any lie, rumour, or half-truth about a politician is "fair game," because we are in the public domain. As a woman, it seems that I am even more vulnerable to the loaded adjectives attached to the "fairer" sex — words like "emotional," "aggressive," "pushy." Ask yourself why an "aggressive Sheila Copps" produces a certain negative image, while an "aggressive Stephen Harper" is seen as signalling a positive turn in his political fortunes.

When things were really tough, it was wonderful to have a big shoulder to cry on. Not only does Austin have big shoulders, he also has an unerring political instinct. He spent most of his life as a labour leader fighting for the little guy. His mother, Stella, a hotel worker herself, actually introduced the first equal pay legislation resolution at a union convention in Newfoundland in 1948, so he came from a family with core people values. With him at my side, and an incredibly supportive family network, I was able to weather the rough moments.

The worst was probably the last year of the 2003 leadership against Martin. Every morning I would wake up absolutely dreading reading the newspaper because I knew the Martin forces were working overtime to leak stories that would destroy me. At one point, my local newspaper had a half-page story about a claim that I had uttered anti-Semitic slurs in front of a mosque. My sister Brenda called me in tears. She knew the story was a lie, but she was so disgusted with the unfairness that she was almost distraught. I immediately initiated legal action against reporter Andrew Dreschel and the *Hamilton Spectator*; the suit is on-going. I have the thick skin to put up with lies but when it hits my family, that makes it really difficult. My daughter, Danelle, was so upset over the nomination process that she literally cheered when I decided that I would not run as an independent in the 2001 election. I tried to use these times in our life to explain that character is like steel. It is forged in fire. It is easy to be a good politician. It is more important to be a good person.

My early days in politics were characterized by a steep learning curve with very few teachers. My family's support was crucial and I also had many friends and political allies who helped me through the toughest times. One of those friends is Henry Lee. I met Henry through our common interest in politics when he came to volunteer on my 1984 campaign. That election was a true baptism by fire. We started twenty points ahead in the polls and ended up just hanging on. In the twenty years since that campaign, Henry and I have shared the highs and the lows. We built the party but we also built a friendship more lasting than any political allegiance. That is the thing to remember about politics. It is more than just a job, it is people bound together by a common bond of values and support. I have friends with whom I worked on my first political campaign in 1977. People like Don Drury and Howard Brown, two devoted Grits who have never been on a Liberal payroll but have devoted countless hours of their life to a party because they believe it can be a vehicle for social change.

When Henry and I first met, he was often subject to racial slurs because his father comes from China. In fact, his father opened the first Chinese restaurant in Hamilton in the mid-1940s. We fought those slurs and we saw Canada change. We saw Hamilton grow as a microcosm of the diversity of Canada. One of my proudest moments in politics occurred following a tragedy. Shortly after the September 11 attacks on the World Trade Center, a Hindu temple in Hamilton was destroyed by an arsonist. In response, the whole community, Christians, Jews, Muslims, and community leaders of all sorts, came together to raise money to rebuild the temple.

During the course of events in the past year, people have often asked me what is it about Hamilton that makes me so proud. *That* is what makes me proud; proud of a community where different people speaking different languages and practising different religions live together. In my toughest political battles, the people of Hamilton never abandoned me. In fact, my experience during the nomination battle reinforced my belief in the basic goodness of people. People from other political parties, people with no party affiliation, called, came in to see me, wrote to show me how much they cared.

Two days after the nomination battle, an older Italian gentleman came into my office. He was having a problem with his pension. I told him I was happy to take up his cause, but he might be better off talking to someone else because I might have to close my office down. He insisted that he wanted only me to solve his problem and he started to cry. That started me going and we cried in each others' arms, sorry together that I would not be there to help him get simple justice. When things were tough in the nation's capital, I always had a place I could call home.

Chapter Five

Cabinet Headaches

One of the things it is very difficult for the average person to understand about politics is that when you are in the opposition, you are all working together toward one goal, the defeat of the government. The salary level for every MP is the same. The official titles are few and far between, so by and large everyone is working together towards a common objective. All of that changes when you get to government.

In fact most government documents make a distinction between Parliament and government that is lost on the average voter but understood by every civil servant. The ministers and the prime minister, the privy councillors and their departments form the government. The Parliament is where the members of Parliament sit, but it is definitely not the government. Most members of Parliament aspire some day to sit in government with a larger salary, as a minister. But once the government is formed, those who are not in the council of ministers can only hope to get there when a colleague fails.

My first clue about the vicious nature of government came in 1993, in the form of an anonymous news story about the day I was sworn in. The story alleged that I had thrown a temper tantrum the day of the swearing-in because my limousine was not immediately ready. Anyone who knows me would realize that nothing could be further from the truth. It's simply not my style. Yet the anonymous source promoting such lies was a portent of what I would come to expect in government. Your colleagues – people on your side of the House – are only too happy to see you fail, making room for them to climb over you.

The first day I arrived in the cabinet rooms, I was struck by encountering the largest bottle of Aspirin I had ever seen. In the anteroom stands a small table filled with drugs and medications of choice – Pepto-Bismol, aspirin, Tylenol, and many more. I remember wondering why we needed all these pharmaceutical products. "Will there be that many headaches in cabinet?" How little I knew. When I entered the inner cabinet room for the first time, I remember feeling the awe of being in a place where all the major decisions affecting my country were made. I could almost close my eyes and conjure up a vision of the great debates that must have taken place in this room. The room itself is not large. Its oak-panelled walls include a portrait of the first leader of the party in power. In our case, Sir Wilfrid Laurier stared down upon our proceedings and we were constantly reminded of the gravity of our responsibility because a quote from the Bible was carved in the wall opposite the prime minister's seat asking us, the rulers of the earth, to seek justice. The cabinet table is oval and the prime minister sits in the middle. This reflects the belief that the prime minister is "first among equals," an interesting concept.

I had spent a decade in Parliament and the previous seven years working in politics, and yet I had no idea what it meant to govern. I was, I think, fairly typical of most parliamentarians who join the government and become cabinet ministers: I was clueless. Government, you see, remains one of the few areas where most of the learning is done on the job and there is even a built-in bureaucratic interest in the Department to keep the Minister in the dark. In fact, if a Minister asks few questions and the bureaucracy gets its work done, the business of government moves along nicely. If a Minister asks too many questions, the system does not work as smoothly as the Ottawa bureaucracy would like. Brilliant politicians, those who know how to get things done, are rare, and their political wisdom often remains private, and leaves when they leave.

For example, Lloyd Axworthy was one of the brightest politicians in my lifetime. He was a brilliant policy analyst. He loved the forward-thinking involved in policy development and also understood the timeworn adage that "all politics is local." He never failed to look out for Winnipeg and if there was an opportunity to bring an advantage to his home community, he snapped it up. Yet when Lloyd left politics, that twenty-five year reservoir of knowledge went with him.

In most businesses, senior executives with his background and intelligence would be called upon to help new ministers adapt to the job. Not in politics. The day Lloyd, or any other Minister, was out the door was the day his successor had to start differentiating himself. New ministers are judged not by their continuum with a predecessor, creating a smooth transition, but rather by their capacity to cut a new swathe, to sever ties, not to build on them.

The other aspect of public policy that made the Aspirins necessary is that each member of the executive branch in the cabinet was there because the governing party had the support of dozens of backbenchers. Many of those backbenchers might well be more talented than the ministers but for reasons of balance, geography or personal ties, they were not chosen. Their chance of getting into cabinet depended on a minister's resignation. When a minister got in trouble, it is safe to say that not every backbencher was unhappy.

In my case, there was a fourth dynamic operating. I had run a surprisingly strong third in a leadership race in 1990, garnering almost half the number of votes earned by Paul Martin, and spending only $800,000 against his recorded amount of $2.37 million. That was significant because he had been campaigning unofficially since 1984 and officially since 1990. His underground campaign included dozens of staffers. Some worked for Earnscliffe, a strategy group known for its close ties to the Martin organizing team. Susan Delacourt's book *Juggernaut* speaks of Earnscliffe's unusually close ties: "Earnscliffe had been given the contract to handle Finance's communications strategy during the Tory government's last month, but it was under Martin that it came to be known as almost an adjunct of the department." Others worked in government relations for various companies that did business with the Department of Finance. It was widely known, however, that many of those working in GR (government relations) had only one job: to support Martin in his campaign and keep the lines of communication open with the Department of Finance.

Even after his 1990 loss, Martin's leadership campaign continued with barely a pause. In John Gray's words: "For a time the Martin supporters stopped shooting, but they never disarmed." His first aim was to make sure his eventual coronation would not be threatened by any potential upstarts. And as the Minister of Finance, at the centre of government, he was in a position to ensure that goal. I remember one of my East Coast colleagues telling me he had promised to support Paul Martin in the 2003 leadership race in return for getting a road in his riding paved. That deal was sealed in 1999. Likewise across the country, he used the combination of the carrot and the stick to ensure that nothing stood between Paul Martin and victory in the next leadership. The carrot, support from the considerable budget of Finance; the stick, threats that if a member of Parliament failed to come on board, they would be purged in their own riding in the upcoming nomination.

It took me a little while to figure out how vicious this battle for the hearts and minds of Liberals was going to be. (I suppose you could ask why someone with my years of political experience could be so naive.) Each of us in the cabinet naturally had dealings with the Department of Finance. Our individual success or failure as a Minister depended on the man who held the purse strings. As Murray Dobbin notes in *Paul Martin CEO*, "Martin's finance department could, in effect, pick off each department one by one with its budget-cutting targets. . . . Martin's role gave him great power not only over his own department, but also over the direction of every other federal department."

It also meant that Finance, aware of all government expenditures and proposals, could use that information to curry favour with journalists who were always hungry to get the scoop. That way, Mr. Martin could shape events to guarantee that no competitor would dare to even challenge him the next time for the crown.

The strategy was particularly obvious in the days leading up to our semi-annual cabinet retreats. The day before the retreat, there would always be a leak to a particularly prominent journalist or two about the Department of Finance's presentation to the cabinet. There would be a concurrent leak about the wild spending habits or unrealistically expensive wish lists of Mr. Martin's colleagues, who would be named. Most of the leaks would be designed to make him look like a frugal, wise administrator while any potential opponent would appear in the most negative light possible. In the Liberal cabinet of the day we had certain so-called right-wing and left-wing thinkers. The group that worked for social justice included some politically savvy Quebecers like André Ouellet, and Atlantic ministers who were struggling to keep their regions afloat like Brian Tobin and David Dingwall, who could both be counted on to speak out for the little person. Like me, they were subject to the "spendthrift" labels being attached by anonymous sources in the Department of Finance.

While I was trying to feel my way around the cabinet and learning my new role as Minister of the Department of the Environment, I was also grappling with the role of Deputy Prime Minister and Chair of the Cabinet Committee on Social Union. There were only two committees that reviewed policy. I chaired one, the Committee on Social Union, while André Ouellet chaired the other committee, on Economic Union. The remaining two cabinet committees, Treasury Board and the Special Committee of Council, were involved in expenditure management and regulatory and legal review. As Deputy Prime Minister, I was responsible for backing up the Prime Minister on all departmental files in Question Period. This meant that I had thirty-two hours per week assigned to government meetings before I could meet with a single Canadian. This made it almost impossible for me to get a reality check, a chance to speak to real people to find out if the government was on track, and the thirty-two hours did not include a single visit to my own riding or any work done across the country to keep Liberal fires burning. No wonder there was such a large bottle of Aspirin at the entrance to cabinet.

The day I was to enter cabinet I received a phone call from Fred Doucet, a neighbour and the former chief of staff to Brian Mulroney. He passed along some of the wisest advice I ever heard in politics. "Sheila, if you don't do anything else, get out of Ottawa." Unfortunately, I ignored his good advice. Wanting to be a good minister and to learn as much as possible as quickly as I could, I spent most of my time buried in meetings. I had to work hard departmentally as Minister of the Environment because the Liberal Red Book had an aggressive agenda on environmental reform; socially because the social policy committee that I chaired was responsible for issues as volatile as health care and national child care; and politically because as Deputy Prime Minister I could be called upon at a moment's notice to be on my feet in the House on an issue affecting any department of the government.

Inside a Committee

I spent the first year immersed in the inner workings of government. (I think it's worth going into these workings in some detail in the pages that follow. If it's too much detail for you, please feel free to skip ahead.) As well as establishing two major policy committees, the Prime Minister would establish ad hoc committees to tackle specific problems. At the start of our mandate in 1993 the most famous of those committees was the Committee on Program Review. That was the committee responsible for determining how we would eliminate the $42-billion annual deficit. The chair of the committee was the president of the Treasury Board, Marcel Masse, and the other members were appointed by the Prime Minister to represent regional and demographic concerns.

Each minister was asked to review the expenditure reductions recommended by their departments with a view to ensuring political oversight. Some ministers made changes. Others merely presented the package proposed by their departments. Then it was up to the committee to determine whether the proposed cuts would be politically palatable, or whether a minister needed to take a second look at expenditure reductions. Finance and Treasury Board reviewed the proposals of each department before they came to our committee. The Minister of Finance served on all committees de facto, although he rarely exercised his prerogative, sending the Secretary of State for Financial Institutions to most of the meetings. The committee chair was supported by a secretariat headed by Suzanne Hurtubise, who went on to become my deputy minister in the next shuffle.

It was in this exercise that we began to see real politics at work. Take the case of Foreign Minister André Ouellet. He made strong arguments that Foreign Affairs had already been cut to the bone and therefore should be left untouched in the Program Review process. Those arguments had already been made to the Minister of Finance, but to no avail. Our job was not to assign the level of cuts required from each department but rather to determine whether the cuts were made in the right places. When André came before our committee, he argued again that the department should not be cut, but in the event that a cut had to go ahead, he offered three areas for potential massive reductions. The first was in contributions to the International Monetary Fund, the second was in cuts to support for international financial institutions like the World Bank, and the third was a decision to end funding for Radio Canada

International, which received half its funding from Foreign Affairs and half its funding from the Canadian Broadcasting Corporation.

The total budget of RCI at the time was less than $15 million, but André knew that the committee would not want to sanction the closing of such an important international voice for Canada. He also knew there was no way Paul Martin would want to sustain massive cuts in our contributions to the World Bank and the International Monetary Fund, since they worked directly with ministers of finance around the world and a budget reduction would reflect badly on him with his peers. So the committee rejected André's recommendations. He stood up with a flourish, announced to the committee that he had done his work and left the room announcing, "Well, if you don't like my cuts, you can apply your own."

Most ministers who did not get agreement from the committee were required to return. Some came back willingly, others with greater reluctance. The case of my friend and colleague Brian Tobin was especially interesting. He was Minister of Fisheries and also a very vocal member from Atlantic Canada. So he proposed cuts in line not only with his departmental priorities but also his regional ones. He proposed to the committee that we get out of the business of freshwater activity in Canada and turn that over to the provinces by closing down most freshwater research and data collection capacity in his department. In his initial proposal, the ocean budget would have remained almost untouched while the freshwater budget would be decimated. As environment minister with an interest in freshwater pollution control, and as minister in an area that employed more than three hundred people at the Canada Centre for Inland Waters (i.e. freshwater work), I could not agree to the plan. I also believed strongly that fresh water would be the most crucial natural resource in the twenty-first century. The Great Lakes border on seven different provincial and state jurisdictions and so I argued that a national strategy just made sense. Brian was asked to go back to the drawing board and review some of his recommendations. As a result, we were able to keep freshwater research capacity intact and we also ensured that the national government remained responsible for legislation and enforcement of pollution violations under the Navigable Waters Act.

In the case of Radio Canada International, the committee was unanimous that it should not be cut. However, André refused to come back to the committee with new proposals. He was invited instead to make an agreement with the Minister of Finance. What they agreed to, apparently with the blessing of the Treasury Board, was that Radio Canada International would be transferred to the Department of Canadian Heritage *with a budget of zero*. Normally when a program moves from one department to another, both departments should agree. In this case my predecessor, Heritage Minister Michel Dupuy, agreed to receive the program with no money. He essentially inherited André Ouellet's headache with the approval of the Department of Finance. André's bold ploy had worked. In threatening to cut the IMF and the World Bank, he had certainly caught the attention of the Minister of Finance, who had no qualms whatsoever about offering up RCI to the unsuspecting Michel Dupuy. Little did I know that when I objected to the closing of RCI, I would inherit the headache as the next Canadian Heritage Minister.

The work of the Program Review committee was long and arduous. Tradeoffs such as the ones I've described were made, and emotions flared as the cruel reality of cutting twenty-five thousand public servants sank in. But there was on the committee a real sense that we had worked together to come up with a series of recommendations that would best reflect the dual political challenges, moving quickly to a balanced budget and making sure that in the process we protected the most vulnerable. The Finance Minister's commitment to fighting the deficit was national legend. But what people didn't know is that every expenditure had been reviewed by a whole team starting with the Prime Minister and including every minister in the government. In fact, the only department where the budget was untouched was Indian Affairs; with the large increase in Aboriginal population, it was impossible to provide water, education, and health for them without significant new dollars.

That being said, the Prime Minister wanted to support his Minister of Finance and he worked very hard to ensure that any restraint from Finance was not undercut by the Prime Minister's Office. Prime Minister Chrétien was very proud of the fact that he had been the first French-Canadian Minister of Finance. He would often bet with Paul Martin on who would be closest on year-end surplus estimates. Chrétien provided to Paul Martin what Michael Wilson never received from Brian Mulroney, and that was the prime-ministerial spine to back up the Finance Minister throughout the fight on the deficit. Chrétien was also particularly sensitive to the angst that could be caused by a prime minister undercutting a finance minister. That had happened to him once with Mr. Trudeau when a major financial decision was made and announced by the PMO without his knowledge, and he vowed he would never inflict such an embarrassment on a successor.

And support him he did. Whenever other ministers would complain to the Prime Minister's Office about the leaks coming from the Department of Finance, the Prime Minister's alter ego,

Eddie Goldenberg, would merely shrug off the complaints as part of the business of politics. At times, the unflagging support for the Department of Finance defied logic. Radio Canada International was a case in point. As soon as I became Minister of Canadian Heritage, I inherited the RCI mess and immediately spoke to the other interested minister, newly minted Foreign Affairs Minister Lloyd Axworthy. We both agreed that this decision had to be turned around. The letters were flooding in because we were cutting off a Canadian lifeline that actually reached 700 million people by shortwave. Lloyd and I worked on a two-fold solution. I was to ask the Board of Directors of the Canadian Broadcasting Corporation, the mother arm of RCI, to fund half the cost of an annual budget, approximately $7 million. Lloyd was somehow to secure the other $7 million internally from Foreign Affairs and we were going to keep RCI open for one year while we explored other options. Both ministries were in agreement, so we assumed the deal was done. Imagine my surprise when at a meeting of the Organization of American States in Bolivia, I received a phone call stating that CBC president Perrin Beatty was on television delivering a verbal dismissal notice to RCI employees within the sixteen-week notice period required under the Canada Labour Code. I was livid. I immediately called the Prime Minister who informed me that the Department of Finance had vetoed our agreement to keep Radio Canada International open because the Minister was afraid that if we changed one Program Review decision the whole process would be compromised. I informed the Prime Minister that the Program Review Committee had rejected the proposal to close RCI down, a decision that was now being unilaterally overturned by the Minister of Finance. I was at the meeting in Bolivia with Clifford

Lincoln and the Honourable Ethel Blondin-Andrew, who were both aghast that once again RCI appeared to be on the chopping block. The Prime Minister agreed to hold off on a decision until I returned to Canada and we had a chance to discuss it in person.

Within forty-eight hours I was back in Canada. I had a meeting planned with the Prime Minister on Wednesday after caucus. In the meantime, I pulled together a team to help us save RCI. Mac Harb, a Lebanese immigrant who knew the international value of Radio Canada, spearheaded the effort. We talked to as many caucus members as possible, with particular attention paid to those who had the ear of the Prime Minister. It was Christmas week on the Hill, when all the parties were celebrating their Christmas dinners, and there was a very important guest at our dinner who definitely had the ear of the Prime Minister. Her name was Aline. Everyone knew her as a loyal and devoted spouse who saw the youthful spark in the little guy from Shawinigan and groomed it astutely and impeccably. She liked to stay deep in the background when matters of state were being considered on the Hill. But she also had a strong social conscience, spoke four languages, and knew the value of RCI to the world. She was a natural to defend it. When I approached her quietly at the Christmas party, she whispered discreetly, "I will talk to Jean." Next morning at caucus, Mac Harb delivered the icing on the cake. Member after member rose from their place to say how important it was to keep RCI. So when I went for my meeting with the Prime Minister, his mind was made up. He was willing to weather the wrath of the Minister of Finance and approve the funding return to RCI. And so we were able to follow through on our commitment to keep Canada's voice open to the world.

Many other decisions of Program Review were not so easy to reverse. Nor did we want to reverse them. What we did want was a general understanding that the work being done to pave the way for seven successive balanced budgets was shared work. Instead, we had a situation where the Minister of Finance managed to convince the Canadian public that he was solely responsible for the health of the country's balance sheet, but every cut was the responsibility of other ministers. Ironically, when Radio-Canada's budget was cut by 25 per cent, a cut that was announced in the budget a few days after I became Heritage Minister in January 1996, I was given the responsibility of explaining the cuts to the journalists. Several budgets later, when funding was restored, the good-news announcement was mysteriously leaked in advance of the budget by – you guessed it – the Department of Finance.

And then there were the proposals for cuts floated by the Department of Finance that thankfully never saw the light of day. One of the proposals Paul Martin floated early in our mandate was to abolish the old-age pension. He came before cabinet to propose that to be truly successful in wrestling the deficit to the ground every Canadian had to feel the pain, including seniors. I remember cabinet members looking furtively at each other, aghast at the idea of a Liberal government abolishing the Old Age Pension as one of our first acts. In fact, André Ouellet, who chaired the economic committee of cabinet, thought the idea was crazy and told the Prime Minister so. I reiterated my concern that cutting the most vulnerable in our society would certainly not be in the interest of Liberalism. Paul Martin came back with figures to show how many seniors were living well above the average income. He argued it made no sense to exclude them from the national belt-tightening exercise since the credibility of deficit reduction meant that everyone had to be involved. In the end, that was one call made by the Prime Minister. He too felt it would be politically damaging and socially foolish, and he stepped in to veto the Martin plan to abolish seniors' pensions.

Martin also thought that the government money going into regional economic development should be abolished. On that one, he faced some pretty stiff opposition from Lloyd Axworthy, David Dingwall, and Brian Tobin, all of whom had personal experience with the challenge of attracting economic investment to people living far from the financial centres of Montreal and Toronto. A horrific fight broke out in cabinet. In the end, regional development funds were not abolished, but they were trimmed substantially with new lending criteria designed to get a better national return on investment.

During this period we were also taking a hard, painful look at employment insurance. Lloyd Axworthy was the minister responsible for Human Resources, a multi-billion dollar department with responsibility for everything from student loans to unemployment insurance. He knew we had to get the finances of the nation in order, but he also felt that by using models of worker empowerment, we might achieve the government's financial objectives without alienating every worker in the country. His idea was to explore the possibility of organizing the workers in sectoral organizations to manage employment insurance funds. At my request, he had begun a preliminary discussion with the national construction unions. A sectoral employment fund could be managed by workers and it could eliminate the underground economy at the same time. Lloyd was conscientious and creative; he wasn't afraid to test out new ideas. He also had the interest of the workers at heart and wanted to create a fund that would be a springboard to new opportunities.

Unfortunately, his interest in innovation bucked up against the Department of Finance's need for financial certainty. They needed to know price tags, and – to be cynical – they especially needed the surplus from the employment insurance fund to go toward debt reduction. So instead of taking a chance with innovation in employment insurance, we cut the average access to employment insurance drastically.

The decision didn't hurt us nationally, but in 1997 the wrath of the voters in Atlantic Canada stung us as riding after riding fell. The changes to employment insurance were cited as the single major reason that political powerhouses like David Dingwall and Doug Young went down to defeat, among other major losses in Atlantic Canada. That year, my husband participated in a sailing regatta and he was on our boat in Dingwall Harbour in Nova Scotia when he called with the news that David Dingwall had gone down. I couldn't believe it and I was afraid that in Ontario we were going to face similar losses. However, the bleeding stopped once we reached Quebec and we were able to cement another Liberal majority, albeit a reduced one.

Deputy Prime Minister on the Road

While we were engaged in the financial re-engineering of government, the normal business of government continued apace. As Deputy Prime Minister I was required to replace the Prime Minister at international events where a senior government presence was expected but he was unable to attend. Among the first of these, and certainly the most moving and memorable, was the inauguration of Nelson Mandela as the new president of the Republic of South Africa. He was not only successful in replacing the apartheid government of F.W. deKlerk; he also inspired the whole world for the more than two decades he spent in custody fighting for the simple principle that all people are equal. DeKlerk helped bring an end to apartheid and remained in the transition government, serving as number three to Nelson Mandela and Thabo Mbeki. I had the privilege of meeting privately with both of them during the inauguration. I also had a chance to witness first-hand a government in transition and a people taking a leap of faith for which there was not unanimous support.

A few days before I left for South Africa I received a briefing from Foreign Affairs. They were worried because bombs had been going off in advance of the handover and they wondered if I had any security concerns. I realized that my only security concern was that I didn't have a will, so I wrote one on the back of a serviette, witnessed and probably not legal, but now in existence, just in case. When we landed in South Africa we were met by a full security escort, which included a combination of crack South African military police and members of Canada's Royal Canadian Mounted Police. (All men and all white.)

The first evening we were feted at a dinner hosted by the local government in Pretoria. The first half of the evening included a goodbye dinner speech by deKlerk. The dessert featured a speech by incoming president Nelson Mandela. I was interested to notice that neither was present for the other's speech. In fact the fear and trepidation in the audience (mostly white) was palpable. I was seated at a table with a local city councillor appropriately involved in the steel business. Welcoming me, he loudly stated that he didn't feel women should be involved in politics because we were too emotional. He followed that comment by saying equally loudly that we were really eating at the Last Supper tonight because the change in government tomorrow would be the end of South Africa as we knew it. He advised me that the only reason this fool-ishness was happening was because of the rand; the continuing political instability was wreaking havoc with their currency. He ended the evening asking me if there was any way I could fast-track an immigration application because he was definitely planning to get out of South Africa, although he thought he would prefer Australia to Canada as a destination. I thanked him for the dinner, wished him well in Australia, and adjourned to my hotel room for the momentous meetings the next day with two men who would later jointly share the Nobel Peace Prize for their courage and vision in ending apartheid.

On the way back to the hotel I had a chance to chat with some members of the RCMP security detail. They had a fascinating per-spective because they were working closely with the South African police and had a chance to talk with their colleagues about the fear they felt about the transition. Here was a police force that had spent years ensuring that the laws of apartheid were upheld, who would now be working in transition for the very people who had been imprisoned because of those laws. They told me their colleagues were holding their breath because they didn't know what to expect. Everyone was hoping for the best but preparing for the worst.

The next day I had a chance to meet in person the two people who had made it possible. Nelson Mandela was incredi-ble. Such an aura of peace and internal fortitude emanated from him that I knew I was meeting with one of the truly great leaders of my lifetime. There were five of us at the meeting, representing the Commonwealth states of the Americas. We spent a few minutes passing along the support of our respective countries and then we listened to his hopes and aspirations. I had wondered what kind of leader he would be. Having spent more than two decades in prison, he had every right to be angry and vindictive toward those who had robbed him of the best part of his adult life. Instead of vindictiveness, I saw reconciliation. Instead of anger, I saw hope.

Perhaps the most symbolic example of that hope was the story of Mandela and his prison guard. One of the most honoured guests at his inauguration was this prison guard, a man who became so attached to Nelson Mandela during his time on Robben Island that he actually asked him to be the godparent of one of his children. When Mandela was finally released from prison, the guard retired, because he said he could never guard anyone as great as Nelson Mandela. His invitation to sit among the honoured guests at the inauguration sent a powerful message. The message was the new South Africa would be built by all its citizens. He would not repeat the apartheid mistake of leaving a whole race out of decision-making in government. He opened his arms to all peoples, all communities.

He even provided a place of honour for those who had built their careers upholding apartheid. As vice-chair of the Standing Committee of Human Rights, I had participated in the parliamentary hearings in Ottawa on apartheid prior to the Canadian government's decision to impose sanctions. In fact, it was our motion on sanctions that eventually formed the basis for the Canadian position, just as in turn Canada set an example for the rest of the Commonwealth. During the summer hearings, the South African government asked for an opportunity to appear.

With the High Commissioner came Chief Buthelesi of the Zulu people, there to support apartheid, suggesting that it reflected the historic tribalism by region that pre-existed the arrival of the Europeans. Yet now Chief Buthelesi, too, was given a place of honour at the inauguration.

Following the Mandela meeting, we had a few free hours before the meeting with deKlerk, so we decided to go over to the office of the African National Congress. This formerly outlawed organization, which had kept the flame of democracy alive for millions of disenfranchised Africans, was soon going to be directly attached to the seat of government. But it had not happened yet. When we arrived in full police escort, our group was greeted with a mixture of veiled skepticism and fear. We could feel how the siren of the police escort meant something chilling to those who had spent years behind bars as a result of their pursuit of freedom. Following our ANC visit, we drove to Soweto for a chance to see the townships. Again the glances that came our way were a mixture of fear and disbelief – disbelief that this moment of freedom had finally come, and fear of the white police who were accompanying our official delegation.

A few hours later, I had a private meeting alone with F.W. deKlerk, the outgoing president who had paved the way for South Africa to abandon apartheid. There were many theories behind his decision. One said that it was a bi-racial romance in the family that turned him around. Whatever the reason, this person who had been elected to preside over the country in a party based on apartheid, was giving it all up. He, too, seemed a quiet, thoughtful man, happy with his decision and prepared to work with the new government to smooth the transition to majority rule. His deep and abiding belief in his country shone through. It could not have been an easy time for him. Reviled by some in his own party, he was also seated at a place of honour at the celebratory meal following the inauguration. Yet as he walked into the tented dining area, I overheard a high-ranking general in the armed forces seated beside us hissing across to his neighbour that he would "love to kill that bastard."

Such was the tenor of the times; utter joy and terror coexisted, and in a seventy-two-hour period, the world came together to witness something that would not be seen again in my lifetime. The attendees at the inauguration were drawn from every corner of the globe and every political persuasion. During his time in prison and through the ANC Mandela had established contacts in literally every part of the globe. Mohamar Ghaddafi was rubbing elbows with Yasser Arafat and Fidel Castro with Al Gore (or at least trying to). In fact, the morning of the inauguration, heads of state and government were gathered for breakfast to await the procession to the event. We arrived approximately two hours before the motorcade began, which gave us lots of opportunities to meet with other countries' representatives. I watched with particular interest the diplomatic tango between Fidel Castro and Al Gore. Castro was anxious to touch base with the Democratic administration in the White House and the White House was equally anxious to avoid him. As Castro moved toward Al Gore to say hello and shake hands, you could literally watch the Secret Service agents whispering in Mr. Gore's ear. With only about four hundred people in the room, it was not difficult to spot Castro and Gore. In fact, it was almost comical to watch how Gore was avoiding Castro and how Castro was pursuing Gore. The two of them spent two hours moving about the room, never to cross paths.

At the appointed time, we all boarded our vehicles and headed to the inauguration. The streets were lined with thousands of people singing and dancing with the energy derived from pure joy. It was almost as though we were in the middle of a million-person conga line and each enthusiastic reveller was outdoing the next. Never, never had I seen such collective joy and abandon on the faces of so many people. It was an unforgettable feeling and certainly among the highlights of anything I will ever experience in public life. If you could ever bottle a day, to say *this is what democracy should mean to us*, it was this day. Tears of joy flowed down the faces of thousands in the streets. A decade later, I still get goosebumps just reflecting on the emotion and history attached to that day.

The inauguration itself took place in the open air with the hot sun beating down on the thousands who were participating officially and the millions who were celebrating in the streets. It was solemn yet joyful, serene yet hopeful. I have had the privilege of hearing Mr. Mandela speak on a few occasions since then, and every time I recall the incredible power that came from his measured words that day. I knew reconciliation would come. I knew also that whatever petty challenges we had in knitting Canada together, none would compare with the challenges of rebuilding a world where a whole population had learned hate and discrimination as a legitimate form of political expression. Shortly after the inauguration and lunch, we boarded a plane to return to Canada. The defining moment of history that I had shared had lasted less than seventy-two hours.

Chapter Six

Not So Easy Being Green

Such moments were sandwiched in between the normal business of government. As Environment Minister, I had a hectic legislative schedule because one of the strongest planks in the Liberal Party platform had been the greening of Canada. That meant we had to tackle tough issues like the changes to the Canadian Environmental Assessment Act, the new rules on toxic substances, and the greening of government. It also meant that we had to start to tackle the problem of global warming. Kyoto may have been a decade away but in 1993 the Liberal Party Red Book promised that we would reduce Canadian greenhouse gas emissions by 20 per cent. I remember asking my deputy minister to begin work on preparing for our 20 per cent reduction and his response to me was "That was politics, this is government." He suggested that it was naive of me to think that just because we promised to do it during the election, it would be done.

I make no apology for taking our Red Book promises seriously. But not everyone in our cabinet did. According to *Double Vision: The Inside Story of the Liberals in Power* by Edward Greenspon and Anthony Wilson-Smith, Paul Martin often yelled at people in the Finance Department who dared to mention it as a source for their policy: "Don't tell me what's in the Red Book. I wrote the goddamned thing. And I know it's a lot of crap."

In fact, I learned very quickly that in politics the public interest so valiantly expressed during elections often falls victim to the private interest in the course of governing.

Nowhere was the private interest more present than in the regulatory regime governing the environment. It was probably the department of the government where the public interest collided most often with established private interests. Even a good platform and a tough minister had to overcome the fact that the nation's capital devoted much more attention to the private interests of lobbyists and corporate interests than it ever could to the public good. Luckily, we were early in our first term and the thoughtful environmental platform prepared by a great research team guided by Chaviva Hosek and co-chaired by Paul Martin, was so well laid out that I was able to move in environmental areas with a speed that rendered the bureaucrats incredulous.

At one point, I was working on the preparation for the Canadian Environmental Protection Act, a sweeping new piece of legislation which involved comment by almost every department. Every time environmental action was proposed, I found that you could assume an immediate negative response from the departments of Finance, Natural Resources, Agriculture, and Industry. Unfortunately, the established economic interests were opposed to *any* toughening of environmental laws and they had a direct line into most of the departments in Ottawa. I always believed that as a minister "my client" was the Canadian people, but after a few months on the Hill it became clear the "clients" who counted were those with established commercial interests. That meant that environmental interests were often trumped by commercial interests. Whenever issues came to the table, the environment minister found himself or herself in a minority. It also made it really difficult to tackle the complicated issue of environmental sustainability. As long as the cost of doing nothing was more attractive to business than doing something, the corporate lobby – especially the oil and gas lobby – would always convince the government that waiting was better than acting.

Such pressure from commercial interests combined neatly with the fact that most provincial governments had a direct line into the Prime Minister's Office, and most provinces would vigorously defend their own corporate interests against troublesome environmental "meddling" by my department. Quebec supported clean Kyoto targets because they had plenty of renewable hydro power. But they could – and would – override environmental concerns to flood areas to improve hydro production. Alberta, of course, was the leader in petroleum production and discouraged *any* regulations to improve the environment.

A curious example of how short-sighted this approach was came across my desk very early in the mandate. Under the Conservative government, with environment ministers like Lucien Bouchard and Jean Charest, the Green Plan and the government's commitment to the environment was well known. Environment was "hot" in political terms, and a billion dollars had been set aside for environmental initiatives. The money was the easy part. It was the carrot, and when it came to problem-solving, governments liked carrots. Programs were created to invest in the environment and promises were made to strengthen environmental law. The money flowed freely. The hard part was the government's decision to crack down on pollution.

The first experience I had with the disconnect between rhetoric and action was on the file on pulp and paper. When Jean Charest was Environment Minister, he passed a series of strict new effluent standards which were scheduled to be implemented when I became the minister. I found that the pressure to delay implementation was enormous. Two of the key pulp-and-paper producers happened to be based in the ridings of David Dingwall and Brian Tobin. They lobbied hard to delay the date for tightening the rules on effluent discharge. The media also did its part to kill the legislation. Stories were printed in national newspapers suggesting there would be wholesale closure of paper mills across the country if the new rules were not delayed. That was the background against which I had to argue the government's promise to go green. During the election we had been very strong on environmental issues. Sounds great in a brochure but when you are faced with the real possibility of thousands of job losses in poor regions of the country, reality strikes. I pursued the green agenda, much to the chagrin of some of my colleagues. In the end, the Prime Minister backed me up and we proceeded with tighter controls on pulp-mill effluent. The new rules actually created some construction jobs during the upgrades and, in the end, not a single job was lost.

Some years later, one of the companies involved in the lobbying effort to stop the new regulations told Fisheries Minister Robert Thibeault that in the end the changes actually saved jobs. When Europe closed the doors to environmentally negative products, Canada was able to claim that our pulp mills had zero effluent and therefore passed the European "green" requirements. Robert was nice enough to let me know about the change of heart by a Nova Scotia company. I appreciated it because, in politics, you often hear complaints about the mistakes you made. You seldom hear thanks for good decisions. In this case, jobs were saved, the environment was cleaned up, and never a positive word was written by those journalists who had predicted gargantuan job losses. After all, they were only printing what the companies had predicted, and there was no onus on anyone to set the record straight.

In fact, most companies were so heavily tied in to Official Ottawa that it was suggested to me early on that as Minister I should get together on a regular basis with the Friday Group. This was a loose-knit group of companies representing the mining, petroleum, and pulp-and-paper sectors that had a particular interest in influencing the environmental direction of the government. I did attend a couple of sessions, until it became clear to me that their main objective was not to promote the environmental agenda but rather to slow it down.

I quickly came to understand that the only way to promote the environment was to make it more expensive to pollute. How do you do that? It is not very complicated. Take the issue of ozone depletion. The reason that people are more susceptible to getting sunburned these days is because of the thinning protective layer surrounding mother earth. The Montreal Protocol, signed by the Conservative government, set the stage for acting to reduce the release of chlorofluorocarbons (CFCs) into the atmosphere. I followed their work with a second meeting in Vienna where we started attaching a real cost to ozone depletion. At that meeting, we set timetables for the replacement of CFCs by HCFCs (hydrochloro-fluorocarbons), which could act as coolants for air conditioners and refrigerants without damaging the environment. Our agreement accelerated the move to more environmentally friendly replacements, but the biggest switch happened when the price started to reflect the real cost. It used to cost a few bucks to top up your air conditioner, so there was absolutely no incentive to treat CFCs carefully. They were often released into the environment with little regard for the proven ozone thinning, or the increased cancer risk. Once the true cost began being reflected, the abuse of CFCs diminished remarkably. We were on the way to solving the ozone thinning problem.

We had dealt with acid rain. We showed that with political will, sustainability was possible. Where the cost of doing nothing was more than the cost of doing something, environmental habits changed and the world went greener. Why then, was it so hard to encourage major environmental change? One of the first things we agreed to following the 1993 election was the establishment of a joint panel between the departments of Environment and Finance to examine the tax disincentives attached to environmentally unsound practices by the government. Our first thought in cleaning up the country was to start with ourselves, the government. If we could review and eliminate all practices that discouraged sound environmental policy, starting with the tax system, we would be well on the way to solving the environmental problems like global warming that were looming in the very near future. Once again, campaign rhetoric ran smack up against reality. Notwithstanding the fact that Paul Martin had co-authored the Red Book and had built a reputation on his environmental concerns, we couldn't get to first base on the study with the Department of Finance. It took us almost a year simply to agree on the membership of the study group, because every name proposed by the Department of the Environment was vetoed by Finance.

One of the key areas of tax policy dealt with the unequal tax treatment accorded to non-renewable fuel extraction; generous exploration credits were available to discover new fossil-fuel sources, but unavailable to people trying to find new methods of *renewable* fuel use. The Department of Finance categorically refused to even consider examining any of these questions in tandem with the Department of the Environment. It was their view that in spite of what the Red Book had said, taxation was the sole purview of the Department of Finance. They had no intention of making major changes in tax treatment.

In the end, after almost two years of frustrating stonewalling by the Department of Finance, we were able to take some baby steps toward sustainability. One measure involved ensuring that recycled lumber was given the same tax treatment as new lumber. Another measure saw the development of an ecological tax credit that permitted people to make donations of virgin land to the Crown for a tax credit. The development of that tax credit, which was first proposed at a Liberal convention by British Columbian Karen Morgan, formed the basis for a new series of land donations which helped us in our promise to set aside 12 per cent of the public lands in Canada for future generations.

That in and of itself was a laudable goal. Once again, the government was prepared to move with the carrot, the tax incentive, but when it came to dealing with the issue of sustainability, we could not get to first base. The insatiable demand for fossil fuel was leading to a generalized warming of the planet. I remember giving a speech early in my mandate that painted a stark picture of the future of the planet if we did not act on global warming. I suggested it was time to begin building a national plan. I also pointed out what the International Panel of Climate Change was predicting if the world did not act. This eminent gathering of scientists from all countries around the world studied the science of global warming, not the politics. They predicted a significant increase in flash floods and forest fires and a significant increase in sea levels that would actually cause some Pacific islands to disappear. The media immediately jumped on my speech as extreme and unbelievable (I still have a copy of an editorial cartoon in the *Globe and Mail* which showed me clinging to the edge of Prince Edward Island as it was disappearing under water). Several years later, Canada is experiencing forest fires the likes of which have never been seen in recorded history, and some island states are already under siege.

Charles Caccia, a former environment minister and great advocate for a true plan on sustainability wisely took me aside and warned me that global warming was to be *the* issue of the next decade. He predicted that this would be the most crucial environmental issue of our lifetime.

First We Take Berlin

I was mandated by cabinet to represent Canada at the first world conference to plan a strategy for global warming, the Berlin Conference (a sort of warm-up for Kyoto). Leading up to the Berlin Conference it became increasingly clear that the forces against a strategy for climate change – the same forces that gathered several years later to fight against Kyoto – were working double overtime within the Department of Finance. Notwithstanding Paul Martin's public support for the environment, he was working directly with two western colleagues, Justice Minister Anne McLellan of Alberta and Natural Resources Minister Ralph Goodale of Saskatchewan, to ensure that Canada's input at the Berlin Conference was as weak as possible.

There was no doubt that reducing fossil-fuel emissions presented particular challenges for Canada on two counts. First, the benchmark year against which levels were to be evaluated was 1990 and Canada had already undergone a period of aggressive emission modernization in the mid-eighties that would only make further reductions more difficult. Secondly, the European Union was in much better shape to achieve its goals. Its 1990 baseline incorporated the emissions of East Germany as part of the German family (where any factory closing or modernization would improve their emission numbers). Under the auspices of the Thatcher revolution on privatization, the United Kingdom had just privatized its coal mines, resulting in major closures, with their concomitant decrease in fossil-fuel emissions.

As Environment Minister, I was working directly with all ministers of the G8 to seek emission reductions. But it wasn't easy comparing our record to Europe's because they had obviously embraced an action plan for reduction while we were still dithering on what form that plan might take. I remember hosting a G8 environment ministers meeting in my hometown of Hamilton where British minister John Gummer singled out Canada as one of the worst offenders in the growth of fossil-fuel emissions. Mr. Gummer was right. Our great size as a country has been a blessing and a curse — a blessing because, unlike the United Kingdom, we have huge tracts of uninhabited land and a sense that the country and its environmental potential is unblemished; a curse because the very vastness of Canada has led to a sense that we don't need to plan our urban living in the same sort of detail as the Europeans. We just keep building out, out, and out with the sprawl, congestion, and fossil-fuel emissions that go along with the North American mentality that the car is king. The Europeans don't have that luxury. At the time Mr. Gummer was chastising Canada, his country on average supported over five hundred people per hectare of land and we supported three. No wonder the Greens were big in Europe and virtually non-existent in Canada. Their arrival in force in the last federal election is proof positive that environmental issues are finally returning to the national radar screen.

We also knew that one of the biggest revenue producers for both federal and provincial tax coffers in Canada is the tax revenue from fossil-fuel production. Is it any wonder the Department of Finance worked as hard as they could to oppose a plan that could have an impact on primary production? Their motivation was not tied to the future challenges of global warming but rather to the present revenue streams of current producers. The reach of the oil patch went deep into Ottawa as dozens of lobbyists wined and dined deputies and assistant deputies on a regular basis. Those lobbyists were working very hard to ensure the failure of the Berlin Conference. Berlin set the stage for the meeting in Kyoto, Japan, which led to the world protocol we know as Kyoto. The oil patch did not want Canada to sign an agreement that committed us to *any* reduction in fossil-fuel emissions. I, on the other hand, was working with a Liberal Red Book commitment to reduce those levels by 20 per cent. I knew we could not reach Liberal nirvana but I also believed that the key to a world consensus would begin in Berlin. To that end, I had to try to get the provinces on side.

Our first federal-provincial meeting on global warming was in Saskatchewan, one of the producing provinces, albeit a smaller player than its neighbour to the west. When I arrived at the meeting, it became clear that the rule of "consensus" in the environmental agenda would mean moving to the lowest common denominator. There was no way that Alberta would agree to *any* reduction in fossil-fuel emissions, so we spent the better part of a day arguing over whether Alberta should have veto power over the rest of Canada. The most vocal critic of the Alberta position was actually Environment Minister Moe Sihota from British Columbia. With the support of fellow ministers Wayne Adams from Nova Scotia, Barry Hicken from Prince Edward Island, and Kevin Aylward from Newfoundland, we were able to get agreement from everyone except Alberta to seek a 5 per cent reduction of greenhouse-gas emissions. This was a major victory because it was the first time a federal-provincial meeting reached an agreement on potential targets for emission. Alberta's minister stomped angrily out of the meeting but the rest of us went home thinking we had made progress. Little did I know the Alberta perspective would dominate all the preparations for the Berlin meeting on global warming. Working hand in hand with the government and industry in Alberta to stop the momentum for reductions was the Department of Finance under the leadership of the Honourable Paul Martin.

When it proved so difficult to follow up on the Red Book promise on tax disincentives I should have realized that the road to Kyoto would be a rocky one. In fact when Charles Caccia predicted we would run up against the powerful anti-environment lobby, I had no idea it would include the government's own all-powerful Department of Finance. The status quo meant no action, and Finance, Natural Resources, and Industry believed their "clients" depended on the status quo. No matter how much we tried to build on the words of the Red Book, the beltway in Ottawa (the government insiders) did not support any action on global warming. The fight started when Natural Resources wanted to take the lead in Berlin. I argued the lead should be taken by the Department of the Environment since Natural Resources' largest "client" was the oil and gas sector, which was lobbying furiously to support the status quo. I was successful in winning the first battle. The Prime Minister mandated me to head the delegation going to the Berlin Conference on Global Warming chaired by German environment minister Angela Merkl.

World hopes were high for the conference. It was being held symbolically in Berlin, the proposed new capital for the combined Germanies. West Germany was one of the European countries with the strongest "green vote" and the meeting stood as a symbol of the road to a real Kyoto. The Canadian delegation was large and consisted of equal numbers of industrialists and environmentalists, each of whom came to the meeting with different objectives. There were three government parliamentarians in the delegation. Two were former environment ministers who commanded huge respect in the non-governmental organization (NGO) environmental community. The third was the parliamentary secretary to the Minister of Finance; David Walker was there to report back to Ottawa, where the ministers of Finance and Natural Resources were working hard to thwart our progress in Berlin.

The conference started out badly. We arrived at the conference centre to be met by protesters wearing gas masks and denouncing Canada as environmental enemy number one. At that point we were being lumped together with the United States as the one region of the world that absolutely refused to reduce our emissions. The first meeting was held with our officials who explained that their strategy was to hang together in a loose-knit coalition of the JUSCAN countries to oppose any reduction. JUSCAN stood for Japan, United States, Canada, Australia, and New Zealand. It was the suggestion of officials that we work with the United States and other like-minded countries to make sure nothing was agreed to. I politely pointed out that the status quo was not the position of Canada and we would be foolish to cling to a view which was so out of sync with the rest of the world. Meanwhile, I received a phone call from Chairperson Merkl. She wanted to see me privately on the second day of the discussions.

The Canadian delegation was badly split. Environmentalists were encouraging us to show leadership and join with the Europeans in setting real targets while industrialists were grimly focused on the fact that we should offer nothing. They also complained that developing countries had pointedly said they would oppose reductions. Their position made the task of emission reduction that much more daunting, since it could only be accomplished by developed countries. Amongst the developing countries, Brazil and China played a leadership role and it was obvious that any movement on their side would have to come from these two countries. We focused our strategy on how to get them on side.

Yet the whole time we were working on getting an agreement, the parliamentary secretary to the Minister of Finance was phoning back to Canada trying to undermine my negotiating mandate. The climate in the Canadian negotiating office got so tense that phone calls were actually being made from outside the room. At one point, I saw David Walker sneak out of our negotiating room to use a phone in the hallway. I followed him. After he completed his connection to Canada, I tore the phone out of his hand. Lo and behold it was Anne McLellan, Alberta's own friend of the oil and gas lobby, on the other end of the line. In the middle of the conference, Anne had gone to economic cabinet committee chair André Ouellet to try to convince him to call a special meeting of his cabinet committee to strip me of my negotiating mandate. I was told point blank by David Walker that the Minister of Finance would never agree to any reductions and that I had no business trying to work with the developing countries and the Europeans to get any agreement on reductions.

I was furious.

After all the work we had done in Canada, getting provincial governments on side, after all the rhetoric in a Red Book co-written by Paul Martin calling for 20 per cent reductions, we were now being stymied on a proposal to agree to *any* reductions. Later that night at my hotel room, I received a phone call from André Ouellet, who wanted to know what the heck was going on. I explained to him that I was merely carrying out the cabinet mandate as chief negotiator and I believed that if any reductions were agreed to, they would be far less drastic than what we had promised in an election less than two years earlier. André went away satisfied, and the emergency meeting requested by Anne McLellan never took place.

Meanwhile, the world negotiations continued apace, with Mrs. Merkl working very hard to keep the developing countries on board. When I met with her the next afternoon, she was very worried. "It looks like this whole thing is going to crater if we can't get China on side," she confided. She asked if I could meet privately with the Chinese delegation to let them know that Canada was going to commit to some reductions, thus breaking the solidarity of the JUSCAN countries. I agreed to the meeting, held in the corridor of the negotiating sessions. I told the Chinese that if they stayed on board, we would be prepared to make some movement in the status quo position we had tabled. I also said that it was unreasonable for them do nothing when their environmental decisions in the next couple of decades would have huge consequences for the planet. It clearly made no sense for us to agree to reductions while our future competitors were bound by no such obligations. It was reasonable, however, to expect that developing countries should not be governed by the same set of commitments that we were agreeing to. After all, the poorest countries in the world had not benefited from the industrial revolution. Much of our prosperity had already come at the expense of the world environment, for which we had to bear some retroactive responsibility.

I actually believed a world agreement on climate change that included the possibility of negotiating reduction emission credits could be a win-win solution for developed and developing countries. First and foremost, it would permit the world to meet our targets in greenhouse gas reductions and thus improve the rapidly deteriorating situation caused by the warming of the planet. That in and of itself should have been reason to move forward. But even if our negotiating stance was governed strictly by self-interest, the possibility of negotiating an emission trading system for technology transfer meant that we could sell our technology abroad and receive credit for our reductions at home. That was the best-case scenario, because without the participation of countries like Brazil and China, any reductions we could make in greenhouse gas emissions would pale in comparison to their emissions growth.

We knew the world was intertwined on an environmental level. For instance, if you examined the simple issue of toxic substances, the unregulated emissions from eastern Europe were finding their way into the Arctic airstream and eventually turning up as polychlorinated biphenyls (PCBs) in the breast milk of nursing mothers on Baffin Island. We knew a Berlin agreement would not solve all these problems. But a Berlin breakdown would make the promise of Rio, where all the countries of the world signed a treaty on global environmental issues, seem not only hollow but even fraudulent. There I was struggling with Angela Merkl to keep the momentum alive while my own colleagues in cabinet were working to undermine me. What was particularly galling was that Paul Martin had gone to Rio. As the Liberal environment critic, he had publicly announced his support for all measures to deal with global warming. Yet now his department and parliamentary secretary were working vigorously to support the oil and gas sector's position that any reduction was impossible.

After my successful corridor meeting with the Chinese, a formal conference meeting was called to bridge the gap between developed and developing countries. Just before we went in, the U.S. State Department representative reiterated their position, which was to agree on nothing, even if that position caused the negotiations to fail. I got the impression they were secretly hoping for failure so that no future action need be taken. I said nothing, knowing full well that no negotiation would be successful if we started from the premise that the status quo would suffice. We entered the room and began the dialogue that would ultimately lead to agreement. Several ministers from developing countries were speaking to support their position that they should do nothing.

All of a sudden, an incredibly articulate woman, the environment minister from Argentina, swept all the naysayers away. She gave a powerful, moving speech in which she said she did not want to tell her children that her country stood by and did nothing while the world was facing environmental crisis. She was willing to work on the idea of a commitment to reductions coupled with a technology transfer agreement, and she urged other developing countries to follow her lead.

This was the breakthrough that we were looking for. The room went quiet and then collectively waited for the response from those of us who needed to put some water in our wine, too. I looked at my American and Australian counterparts. They were silent, offering no change in the status quo position. The Japanese, too, were unbending. I knew this was the moment where the negotiations could break down forever, ending the possibility that we would ever get to a world solution on global warming. So at this point I took a deep breath and indicated Canada's wish to speak. I announced that given the flexibility shown by developing countries and in particular their openness in accepting their responsibility in being part of the solution, Canada would move away from our commitment to the status quo and agree to support a reduction in greenhouse gas emissions as a show of good faith to keep the negotiations alive. Nothing, nothing was more important than emerging from Berlin with a common objective of reducing greenhouse gases. The room seized the moment and we managed to bring the Chinese back to the table to continue working on a common Berlin Agreement.

The United States was furious. They had no intention of moving on any reductions. Along with other members of the JUSCAN pact, they looked increasingly isolated. (Ironically, not very long after this meeting, President Clinton decided to move very aggressively on global warming and exceed the targets set in Berlin.) At this particular meeting, the State Department was not very happy but the Europeans, led by Angela Merkl, were ecstatic. We managed to keep the momentum going in spite of the American opposition. The German delegation was especially grateful since Canada's intervention at a key moment actually rescued what was almost certain to be a conference ending in defeat.

Mrs. Merkl's personal gratitude also helped us solved another Canada-Europe irritant on the environment. Canada and Europe had long been at loggerheads over the issue of wild animal trapping for fur. Europe's limited natural areas meant that most of their fur industry was dependent on farmed fur. Their capacity to harvest wild animals was almost non-existent. That, coupled with a particularly strong environmental movement that sometimes confused the issues of sustainability and wild harvest, meant the European Union was about to vote soon on whether the types of traps used in trapping wild animals would be banned. Such a ban would mean the livelihoods of thousands of Canadian trappers would be devastated, since Europe would no longer allow the importation of clothing made from these natural furs.

We had already seen what the power of an illogical lobby could do to destroy the seal hunt. Thousands of seals are going unharvested because ill-informed environmentalists have mistaken theatre for good environmental policy. Of course a seal is a beautiful creature with large dark eyes crying out to be saved. But so too is a lamb, a beautiful vulnerable animal led to slaughter merely to feed humans. Logic did not enter into the debate.

I remember once attending a world conference on the environment where Canada was roundly attacked for hunting wild animals with these terribly cruel traps. A member of the European Parliament attacked me in a debate in Japan, claiming that Canada's policies on sealing and trapping were inhumane. I countered with the question, "If you were an animal, which would you find more cruel, living a free life roaming the wilderness only to be trapped and killed in the last twenty-four hours of your life, or living your whole life in the crowded quarters of a tiny stall provided to you by your captors? Which torture would be preferable?" He became silent when he realized the world conference had a broader point of view than that usually heard in Europe. As I was told by my European political contacts, it just wasn't worth it to anger the European environmental movement.

As environment minister, I always believed that sustainable harvesting, even of seals, was consistent with a policy that protected endangered species but made decisions based on good science, not PETA-like hysteria. My husband's father had also been a fisherman and a sealer and I know how many of the coastal and northern families survived from year to year on the little extra they could make from sealing. So I made it my business to do my best to help orient the European debate toward the real issues of wilderness and sustainability.

When I found out the European Union was about to abolish the leghold trap, I approached Minister of International Trade Roy MacLaren to see if he could provide any advice as to how we might influence the European debate. His reply, "Sheila, I am a vegetarian, so as far as I am concerned, all meat should be banned," was not encouraging. I decided to work through the European environment ministers. When they came to Canada for a G7 environment ministers meeting, I also invited the European Commission's Environment representative. I knew there would be opportunities for private discussion outside the glare of European television cameras that might permit a more rational discussion. On the second night of our meetings in Hamilton, I arranged for a presentation from the people of the Six Nations

Territory just south of Hamilton. They explained the reality of Aboriginal life in Canada with a special emphasis on the history of the use of wild fur, predating the arrival of the Europeans by several hundred years. This was part of their heritage, they explained, and they had nurtured the wilderness with such care that it was bountiful and sustainable until the arrival of the Europeans. At the end of the dinner, each minister was presented with a fur hat to take home with them.

That was step one, softening up the Europeans. But step two was much more complicated. It involved turning around the European Parliament on an issue for which there were very few vocal advocates for the Canadian position. This is where Angela Merkl became a critical part of the solution. Her boss, German Chancellor Helmut Kohl, was a very important player in the European Union. In fact, his support could be crucial in our fight to permit Canada's fur garments to continue to be imported into Europe. At the Berlin meeting, I asked Angela if she could do me a special favour. I knew the Chancellor was going to be visiting Canada and I wondered if she could convince him to put the Arctic on his schedule during the trip. She agreed to try. I went home with twin objectives: to continue working toward a real action plan to reduce greenhouse gases and to convince the PMO that the trip by the Chancellor should include a foray into the Arctic.

Much to my surprise (or perhaps not, given the backroom activities of the departments of Finance and Natural Resources in my absence) our work in saving the Berlin Conference was not acknowledged when I returned to Canada. Rather, a campaign to get me out of the environment portfolio was launched by the very industrialists who were so tied into the Ottawa lobbying scene. (Their mouthpiece in the media was Terence Corcoran, a *Globe and Mail* columnist, now with the *National Post*, whose disdain for anything environmental spewed from his columns. His was the column that insisted, long after the world had come to a consensus that global warming was real, that it was merely the figment of some overzealous environmental imaginations, "junk science" in his words. As the insurance industry began to feel the pinch from climate-induced cost increases, and to raise their rates accordingly, he continued to insist that the world was wrong and the oil patch was right.) A particularly vicious letter, signed by most of the people that the Department of Finance had sent to Berlin to lobby against the agreement, found its way to the office of the Prime Minister, attacking me for being too friendly to the environment and not pro-business enough. Imagine, a minister of the environment being pro-environment! Now, there's a novel concept.

"To Get Along in This Town"
Returning to Canada, I knew I would have to fight an uphill battle in continuing to follow the plan laid out by the Red Book. One aspect of the Red Book dealt with environmental assessments. Until I became the minister, the legislation for environmental assessments was a patchwork of jurisdictions and contradictions. In 1993 we had pledged to bring in a new environmental assessment act, something that even Lucien Bouchard had tried and failed to do in his time as environment minister. I found that the people in the ministry were skeptical. I remember one assistant deputy saying to me: "Minister, I have outlived seven of your predecessors and I expect I will outlive you. I have to get along in this town."

Translation: *any proposed legislation had to have the blessing of Finance and Natural Resources or it could not go ahead.* When I teamed up with other ministers, we could sometimes ensure that environmental assessments were top priority, but usually any economic imperative overshadowed the issue of sustainability. I was, however, often able to work with Indian and Northern Affairs to ensure that economic benefits from work in the north was examined in the environmental process. The Honourable Ron Irwin worked very hard to ensure that any project under his jurisdiction was subject to the proper due diligence because the environmental assessment laws also analyzed socio-economic benefits. Ron was a real Liberal in every sense of the word and he wanted to squeeze any economic benefit he could for northern and aboriginal peoples. He also had a very close relationship with the Prime Minister, which helped when fights erupted with other departments. When a company named BHP applied for a license to begin drilling for diamonds, I was under tremendous pressure to short-circuit the environmental process and permit the drilling. Luckily, it was with the help of Ron Irwin that we were able to do a thorough environmental analysis *and* get better aboriginal job guarantees. I remember being criticized for the time taken for the environmental review until I reminded BHP that "diamonds are forever." It did not make me popular with the company, but Ron and I actually extracted more long-term benefits for Canadians because of the proper review process. That was one positive example of the marriage between sustainable development and the environment.

Because we had not dealt with the tax disincentives to sound environmental practices, the pressure to ignore environmental laws was always great. Economic development overshadowed environmental protection. Even when laws were in place, they were often ignored. Such was the case in a very famous court decision on Alberta's Oldman Dam. The previous federal government had refused to intervene in the environmental assessment process, even though the law clearly stated that where federal funds were spent, the government had a duty to participate in the environmental assessment process. The construction of the dam was appealed to the courts, who ruled the federal government was in breach of our own laws. That backdrop set the stage for an overhaul in environmental legislation. The overhaul was to be discussed at a federal-provincial environment meeting in Haines Junction, Yukon, that would go down in the folklore of environmental history.

In introducing the federal legislation, I established a "single-window assessment process" with specific time limits. That was intended to assuage the legitimate fears of project proponents that environmental assessments by one government could take years, only to be repeated by another one. I believed certainty and time-lines were important factors in any business decision and would go a long way in convincing companies that the process was fair.

Soon after the legislation was passed, however, the new buzz-word was "harmonization." In principle, harmonization sounds reasonable. In practice, Alberta led the charge on a harmonization proposal which would have guaranteed that we always ended up with the least stringent harmonized laws. Unbeknownst to me, my deputy and the provincial deputies had been working together to sign an agreement that would have meant a reduction in environmental regulation. The proposal was presented to me on the plane on the way to Haines Junction. I refused to endorse the plan, saying it made absolutely no sense that only months after a new national law on environmental assessment passed, this proposal seemed destined to replace national environmental assessments with weaker provincial laws. There was nothing stopping provincial governments from joining a national environmental assessment to avoid duplication. The real issue was that national environmental reviews were objective and could not be short-circuited by political expediency or corporate pressure.

I was angry that my deputy had engaged in a harmonization discussion with the provinces without even finding out whether I supported the direction. I didn't. I told him that I would not be proceeding with the proposal and he could advise provincial deputies that no harmonization agreement would be coming out of this meeting. I then returned to my motel room, only to be woken at midnight by a call from my deputy. He had been having a drink with other deputies and thought they had worked out a compromise position. Would I mind getting together with him to discuss it? At this point, it became clear that I was being steam-rolled into accepting a principle that I did not believe in. I told him there was no way I would be signing any document, and I would see him in the morning.

The morning came and the atmosphere in the room was tense. Alberta minister Ty Lund had come to the meeting expecting that the government of Canada would be handing over the reins to him on Alberta environmental assessment. Once again, I had a few allies to count on favouring a strong federal position; Nova Scotia, P.E.I., Newfoundland, and British Columbia. At this point, Quebec was only there as an observer, because the new Parti Québécois government did not fully participate in fed-prov meetings (as they were called). But the combined opposition of Alberta, Saskatchewan, and Manitoba, each of which was at that time involved in controversial environmental assessments for pulp and paper mills or uranium developments, sent a clear message. They had no intention of allowing the government of Canada to oversee their environmental process. "Harmonization" was code for abandoning federal environmental assessment law to provincial jurisdiction. At one point in the discussion I asked them the real question, "Who speaks for Canada?" and the silence in the room spoke volumes about the answer. After a pregnant pause, Wayne Adams of Nova Scotia pointed out that someone needed to represent supra-provincial interests.

Ironically, in the Oldman Dam decision that rapped the federal government's knuckles, the construction of the dam was approved by one province with a direct effect on the flood plain and water table of another province and northern U.S. states, all of which had no input. Hence, the need for national environmental assessment. When it comes to environment, what happens in one province has a definite effect on another.

I had the full support of the environmental movement, but I certainly had little support from provincial governments and the industrial community. Even when there was a clear case for the government to act, the influence of the oil patch and the Department of Finance was always heavy-handed. The story of MMT was a case in point.

MMT is a fuel enhancer added to gasoline that was the subject of controversy in the 1990s. The United States had already banned its use, and we joined Bulgaria among the very few countries in the world that still permitted it. As Environment Minister, I was petitioned by the automakers, who wanted MMT banned, having come to the conclusion that the additive was gumming up the pollution-control systems on their cars. I arranged a meeting between the oil patch and the automakers and suggested they take one year to come to a solution which was mutually acceptable, or I would act. One possibility was offering consumers a choice of one MMT-free pump at each station to protect their pollution-control devices.

One year passed. The oil patch did nothing. I moved to legislate, against the objections of my deputy. He advised that I had no grounds and would face a challenge from the U.S. on freetrade grounds. Since the Environmental Protection Agency of the United States had already banned the substance and since I had many consultations with Carol Browner of the E.P.A. before moving on the legislation, I was confident we would not be challenged on trade grounds. I was less confident, however, about being able to withstand the incredible lobbying power of the Canadian-American oil patch. When I moved forward on the legislation, I worked with Marc Nantais of the Canadian Motor Vehicles Association, with the strong support of the automakers. They did their best, but they were a small operation, and no match for the muscle of the Canadian Petroleum Producers Institute. I pushed ahead because it was the right thing to do.

We were getting clobbered on the business pages of the national newspapers. Terence Corcoran was waging a one-man battle against our initiative, and the automakers did not seem to have a counter strategy. At one point, I called up Maureen Kempston Darkes, the first woman president of General Motors and the chair of the Big Three automakers groups, to let her know that without the real muscle of the auto industry, our MMT legislation was dead.

Most interesting of all, I was also facing huge resistance in the bureaucracy of my department. The day I changed portfolios, I was literally on my way to the swearing-in when I called my successor, Sergio Marchi, to advise him to hang tough on MMT because his bureaucrats would surely try to abolish the legislation as soon as I left. He called me back about an hour after the swearing-in. The first item raised by the bureaucracy was – you guessed it – MMT. To his credit, Sergio hung tough and supported the legislation. It wasn't until his successor took over, in a sultry summer cabinet meeting attended by barely enough people to make quorum, that the controversial legislation was overturned. I remember shaking my head when I heard the news, and reflecting on the prescient words of the assistant deputy. "Minister, I have outlived seven of your predecessors and I will outlive you. I have to survive in this town." Truer words were never spoken. I left the portfolio and he stayed on to serve two more ministers.

Chapter Seven

The GST a.k.a. The Get Sheila Tax

That's what they called it in the Finance Minister's inner circle. Paul Martin knew the Goods and Services Tax brought in by Mulroney's government was hated by Canadians and hated by Liberals. He knew the whole party, including the Prime Minister, had gone on record in opposition to the GST. He also knew that a few of us, myself and John Nunziata in particular, had been particularly vociferous about the need to ensure that the campaign platform included abolition of the GST. He also knew that financially it was very tempting for a government to keep such a rich revenue stream flowing. As the Leader of the Opposition, Jean Chrétien, a former finance minister himself, was also hesitant in promising to abolish the hated tax. He had been in government and knew that sometimes what you revile in opposition is actually part of a bigger picture that makes good government.

With the Leader and the future finance minister offside, an initial decision was made to downplay the plan to abolish the GST in our election platform. Some of us, however, worked very hard in caucus to ensure that abolition of the GST would be a full part of our election platform. We had a raucous caucus meeting, with the majority of members demanding a clear position on the hated tax. Some of us were particularly outspoken because in Opposition we had been very hard on the hapless Mike Wilson regarding this insensitive tax that would hit the working poor. So at the end of the caucus meeting, Mr. Chrétien said he was going against his own political instincts but would follow the will of the caucus by ensuring that GST abolition formed an integral part of the 1993 platform.

It was obvious from the beginning, however, that the Prime Minister and the Minister of Finance were lukewarm when it came to the wisdom of promising to abolish a tax that was bringing in $17 billion worth of revenue in its first year of implementations. I, however, was still idealistic and naive enough to believe that what we campaigned so vehemently against in Opposition could not be ignored in government. I still had not grasped the message given to me by my deputy minister, a message that clearly resonated throughout the bureaucracy: "That was politics. This is government."

Trapped by Peter Mansbridge

Those who had previously served in government understood that sometimes election or campaign promises were reviewed "in the fullness of time." Do you remember our impressive promise to have a national child-care strategy in place as a top national priority following the 1993 election? The fine print in that promise required the national strategy to gain the support of all provincial governments. We knew this was unlikely to happen, so we were free to ignore the promise following the election, blaming inaction on the provincial governments.

There was no such escape clause for the GST. And I drew the unlucky short straw of being the Liberal representative on a CBC town-hall debate where the hated GST was the focus of national attention. The debate was part of a series leading up to the election. The Liberals were on a roll. Kim Campbell's temporary bubble had burst. Her party's decision to run those tasteless ads emphasizing the facial deformities of our leader had made things worse for the Tories, and it looked like we were poised for a win. The big MO, momentum, was on our side, so we weren't about to let the hated GST break our rhythm, although some critics had noticed that our leader tended to hesitate on the campaign when asked specific questions about our abolition plans. I was well briefed and instructed to be as positive and tough as possible: we were going to replace the GST. So there I went, Daniel into the Lions' Den, with Peter Mansbridge as the chief lion. Of course, it was one of the usual CBC round tables, with so-called ordinary people actually handpicked from various interest groups, and deft at pinning their victims. The most deft was Peter Mansbridge himself. Someone asked me the question I was dreading, "What will you do about the hated GST?" I responded by saying we would abolish it. Whereupon Peter spoke up, his hands folded and his head tilted in disbelief, egging me on by saying that I knew we would never get rid of the GST.

It was at that point, a few days before the election, that I drove the stake through my own heart. I stated emphatically that I had so much confidence in our commitment to abolish it, that I would personally resign my seat if we formed the government and failed to follow up on our promise. Great applause. The debate ended on a high, I breathed a sigh of relief, and the Liberal team continued to build momentum for the win. The intemperance of my comments would not come back to haunt me for almost three years because that was the amount of time the Prime Minister had given to the Department of Finance to come up with a replacement for the tax.

Cabinet Disputes

In fact, one of our first cabinet meetings gave me some hope that we actually would abolish the hated tax. Paul Martin came to cabinet armed with what we called in the cabinet vernacular a "deck." A deck was an overview of the situation prepared by the bureaucracy for ministers to discuss. A deck meant discussion, while an MC or Memorandum to Cabinet meant a subject was before cabinet for a decision. Following an MC would be a Record of Decision or RD, showing the result of the discussion for implementation. In fact, ministers had to closely watch the drafting of an RD because sometimes a small change in wording could produce a completely different meaning from what the discussion had intended. At this point in our tenure, I didn't understand the difference in the nature of the discussion.

That was a pity because the message from the Prime Minister that day was very clear. Mr. Martin had spent the better part of an hour outlining the government's dire financial situation and explaining the major revenue streams that came in from the GST. He also explained how difficult it would be to abolish the GST because the systems for implementation were so complex it would be akin to unscrambling an egg. Having waited silently throughout the long presentation, the Prime Minister ended the discussion with an impatient review, saying, in effect, of course the Department of Finance is going to say they can't find a replacement. And of course it is going to take some time. But don't say it's not possible. Just get on with it and bring us something concrete.

I was relieved and, in my ignorance, hopeful that the Department of Finance would do just that, return with a series of options that would permit us to follow through on our promise to replace the GST. I should have known, however, that no presentation to full cabinet from Finance Minister Martin could have been presented without being reviewed by someone in the Prime Minister's Office. I knew that Eddie Goldenberg, who worked closely with the Department of Finance, was very much in favour of leaving the GST, since he had been among those strongly advising Mr. Chrétien not to touch the GST during the election campaign. The Prime Minister saw the whole thing as problematic, and as time passed it became increasingly clear that he was not too interested in unscrambling the egg.

Soon bets were on in the caucus. There were those of us who clung to the notion that the Department of Finance would come up with a solution. After all, a replacement transfer tax with a new name that exempted books, home-heating fuel, and a couple of other necessities, would permit us to follow up on our election promise without compromising the revenue stream that had, in effect, replaced the manufacturer's sales tax. Our numbers were becoming smaller, however, as it became clear to Paul Martin's people that the best alternative for his long-term political agenda was no change. After all, more revenues helped him meet his goal of aggressive deficit reduction followed by successive balanced budgets. At the same time, the government member most closely associated with the promise to abolish the GST was me. And anything he could do to undercut any potential rival was in his long-term best interest.

So the government continued for two years with no GST replacement and no MC on the subject. I kept asking Peter Donolo, the masterful spinner for the Prime Minister, what our strategy would be in the event that the three years passed with no replacement. I could not get a straight answer from Peter, which was unusual, because I had always found him to be a straight shooter. Instead, the answer hit me straight between the eyes on the day Paul Martin called a press conference to apologize to Canadians. I was left watching the press conference in disbelief. In one sorry statement, Martin had managed to sideswipe the Prime Minister and hang me out to dry. The PM was sideswiped because he had repeatedly refused to apologize (Susan Delacourt's book has Chrétien telling Joe Fontana a few days later, still furious, "That [expletive deleted] apology. That [expletive deleted] Martin."). I was hung out to dry because, without even picking up the phone to let me know what he was planning, Martin had pinned me into a corner. The GST decision thus fulfilled two functions, an ongoing revenue stream for him and a chance to Get Sheila.

And Get Sheila they did. Or tried to. One of the things that Martin achieved masterfully during the years when he was forming a "shadow government" to Prime Minister Chrétien was to avoid ever speaking ill of a single member of the Liberal caucus; instead he had a significant number of surrogates ready to do it for him on command. Martin made his statement mid-week. I was scheduled to hold a press conference the next day on copyright. We contemplated the possibility of cancelling the conference but decided to go ahead with it. Of course, no one in the press was interested in copyright. They all were interested in what I would do, now that the infamous GST had not been replaced. The *Globe and Mail* was, as Susan Delacourt wrote, "relentless in its calls for Copps's resignation, running a daily editorial." Would I resign my seat, as promised? I lamely stated that a by-election would cost about half a million dollars and then went on to restrict the press conference to questions about copyright.

The following day, there was a major break when I was thrown into a whirlwind tour with the Prince of Wales, who came to my hometown of Hamilton. We travelled together for two days in Ontario and Manitoba, where he designated a new national park. I obviously couldn't explain to Prince Charles why I was being booed in my own hometown, but he quickly picked up the nuances of what was happening and without commenting on the politics of the GST, he sympathized with the difficulties of meeting public expectations in an ever-changing world. He seemed so human and open, not at all like the image that had been portrayed in the press; at one point, he even asked me how I had weathered a divorce and remained a public figure in Canada.

He was particularly interested in two subjects that were dear to my heart: heritage architecture and holistic medicine. I told him about a project I was working on, to see McMaster University and the nearby Six Nations community combine to establish a complementary holistic – traditional medicine unit in a conventional university. Not only was he fascinated by an integrated approach to health, it seemed that he had evolved an integrated approach to life. He was a strong advocate of natural farming and he understood the importance of preserving architectural heritage, as the writings of Jane Jacobs had long explained to North American urban planners.

In fact, it was the influence of his visit in 1996 that led to a proposed tax incentive on heritage preservation that I spearheaded and that was finally announced by John Manley in his one and only budget. The tax incentive was simple, and indeed had been adopted in the United States some three decades earlier. It basically put heritage development on a level playing field with new development by allowing write-offs for a percentage of the costs associated with heritage restoration. A paper produced for the Department of Finance showed the measure would be revenue neutral, because the majority of restoration activity would be in devalued core areas that would become productive only as a result of the restoration. Canada was the only country in the G8 to have no national heritage policy and Prince Charles was shocked to discover that we could actually tear down the Parliament buildings with no legal impediment.

I travelled with the prince for the better part of two days, and on Friday night I said goodbye and made my way to a Liberal Party convention in Windsor, Ontario. The weekend was chock full and I did not have a chance to see my husband until Sunday night. At the convention I was getting all kinds of advice, with most people advising me to hunker down and weather the storm. The one person who called me with a different perspective was Brian Tobin. He told me candidly, "Sheila, if you ever want to have a future in politics, you must step down." It was advice I very much appreciated. Jeffrey Simpson wrote a column in the *Globe and Mail* saying he would jump off the Parliament buildings if I resigned my seat. The Prime Minister wanted me to stay the course, but I did not want to give any indication of my intention until I made up my mind.

On Monday, having discussed the matter at home, I walked into Question Period and the front bench was empty, giving me no chance for a quiet word with the Prime Minister. On Tuesday morning I walked into cabinet and slipped into my usual spot beside him. I whispered in his good ear that he should not say that I would be sticking around. He looked at me, and we set up a meeting for later that day. The press was gathered in hordes outside the office of the Prime Minister on the third floor, a sure sign they thought a meeting was coming up. Getting word of their presence, I phoned the Prime Minister to tell him I would not be coming down in person but wanted to let him know that I had decided to resign and put my case before the people of Hamilton East. He asked me to rethink my position, and I told him my mind was made up. "If I have only one thing in politics," I explained, "it is my name, and my name means honesty. I am not about to destroy my reputation by refusing to do what I promised to do before the whole nation." As a fallback, he asked me to perform an overnight rolling survey in the riding. I agreed, although I never conducted it. I called my riding president and told him to prepare for an announcement in Hamilton the next day.

As I was making my announcement in my constituency, the Prime Minister was advising the caucus. And lo and behold, the first person out of caucus to attack me was Paul Martin's mouthpiece Roger Galloway, followed closely by two other Martin proteges, Shaughnessy Cohen and Mary Clancy. Roger lost no time in blaming me for taking until Tuesday to talk to my husband, my family, and my leader. Paul Martin had taken almost three years to devise his strategy and I had three working days. But in the minds of the Martinis (as they were called on the Hill) any chance to wound a potential opponent was not to be missed.

The by-election was vitriolic. Reform Party sympathizers masquerading as members of the "non-partisan" National Citizens Coalition flew in from across the country. Alberta newspapers were actually funding advertising campaigns urging the people of Hamilton East to defeat me. At one point, I remember knocking on doors on Beach Boulevard when a man started chasing me down the street, loudly accusing me of letting in all the war criminals after the Second World War. I pointed out that I was born in 1952, so it would be pretty hard to blame me for post-war immigration activities.

The campaign was so bad, in fact, that local people saw through the advertising and the organized backstabbing that was going on. The Reform Party had gone so far as to hire a billboard outside my constituency office with a giant pig named Sheila on it, the pig representing me at the public trough. Ugly stuff like that created a public backlash which actually saw my margin of victory rise. Even then the Sun Media chain published an editorial cartoon depicting all Hamilton East voters as asses, with me being the biggest ass of all. I thought that cartoon spoke more about the disrespect for democracy of the Sun Media chain than it did about the voters. In the end the voters are always right, but no matter how often editorial writers espouse that in their columns, it is seldom reflected in their prose. I am still waiting for Jeffrey Simpson to jump off the Parliament buildings; my hopeful daily vigil continues.

Chapter Eight

Deputy Prime Minister

Three little words. Three little initials even, that would catapult me into the centre of things. As the first woman to become the deputy prime minister, I had the added responsibility of "making it" for all women. But I also faced the added cynicism of a Press Gallery that was not empowered when it came to gender balance or even sensitive to recognizing its own narrow, one-gender view. One of the first articles on my appointment set out to show that I wasn't really a DPM, I was just a skirt put there to fulfill gender expectations. The article, if you can believe it, was all about the size (I guess in politics size matters) of my office, and its location.

The office location story is interesting. Very shortly after being named DPM, I was asked by the whip, Don Boudria, to consider trading offices with the Honourable Herb Gray, who had been named Solicitor General and Government Leader in the House, which meant that he needed to be close to the action, across from the entrance to the House of Commons. Normally, as DPM,

I would have inherited the office of Don Mazankowski which was directly opposite the House, but the whip suggested that it would make more sense to have his operations and those of the Government Leader in the House integrated. I agreed. In return, I moved to a beautiful office on the fifth floor overlooking the front lawn and the Eternal Flame. Paul Martin had an office of exactly the same size right next door to the east, and Preston Manning occupied the office to the west, hardly slouch quarters – in fact, my immediate predecessor as a tenant was the Right Honourable Brian Mulroney.

Imagine my surprise to wake up one morning and read in the newspaper that my job as deputy prime minister was in name only because my office was squirrelled away in an obscure corner on the fifth floor. Never mind that the Finance Minister was right next door, in a mirror image of my quarters. Similar disparaging terms were used frequently by journalists who had great difficulty in using "woman" and "deputy leader" in the same sentence. While I was travelling the world, establishing a world network on culture, I went to many remote corners of the globe to convince countries to join the movement in support of cultural diversity. French-language journalists, understanding the challenges attached to being a minority in a sea of anglophones, covered the issue well and substantively. In English, the coverage was non-existent or hostile. The only thing that seemed to interest the *Ottawa Citizen*, for example, was the cost of my travel. When I was invited to the World Association of Journalists meeting in Brazil to speak to reporters from around the world about the issues of diversity and monoculturalism, more than two thousand attended a conference at which I was the keynote speaker. Coupled with the conference was a meeting with the minister of foreign affairs and the minister responsible for culture. Brazil was a key player in Latin America and getting their support on the creation of a world network on diversity would be crucial. Yet the *Citizen* was apparently only interested in how much it cost to fly me to Brazil and back.

Two Very Different Funerals

Ironically certain columnists characterized my job as simply going to funerals (ergo unimportant); some, of course, were the same journalists who excoriated Prime Minister Chrétien when he missed the funeral of the King of Jordan. I actually only attended two funerals outside Canada in the four years I served as Deputy Prime Minister, but they were two of the strangest funerals I've ever seen. One was for former United States president Richard Nixon. It was held in his home at Loma Linda, California, in the presence of every living president, Republican and Democrat. In typical California fashion, it was an outdoor affair, relaxed, casual and oh, so Hollywood. The service was held in the shadows of President Nixon's childhood home and his presidential library.

Unlike Canadian governments, which literally bury their past, each retiring president is given a budget to establish a library. As minister of Canadian Heritage, I established legislation to protect the gravesites of all of our prime ministers. Until that happened, we let our former prime ministers lie, in some cases, in a bed of weeds. Our prime ministers' archives are kept by the state through the Library and Archives of Canada, but, sadly, most of their material is available only to scholars and elites with special access. Jean Chrétien's planned Canada History Museum would have tried to change that, but as part of his effort to obliterate his predecessor's history Mr. Martin cancelled the project. Taxpayers will still be on the hook for the archival material of prime ministers: it just won't be as available to the public.

In any case, Mr. Nixon's memorial service was nestled in between his childhood home and his presidential library. U.S. government does many things very well. Protocol was not one of them. Kings and potentates had travelled from around the world, but the memorial service had run out of plastic lawn chairs. So they were left cooling their heels in the rear while the cast of characters from Watergate was given top billing, so that convicted criminals like G. Gordon Liddy shared front-row seats with international dignitaries like, well, Red Skelton. The most memorable part of the service was the lineup of speakers. Everyone from the governor of California to every living president to Henry Kissinger was asked to pay tribute to the fallen president. Most mentioned the highs and politely avoided the lows, giving a one-sided picture of the man that did not reflect who he was in life and death. By far the most brilliant and direct tribute came from Henry Kissinger. Knowing the President intimately and after living many of the ups and downs of his career with him, he was able to capture the essence of who Richard Nixon was better than any Anthony Hopkins movie, so that I was left with the sense of being in the presence of greatness, however fatal the flaws that accompanied that greatness. In fact, a quote attributed to Richard Nixon is one which neatly describes the ongoing struggle for political survival. "Just because I'm paranoid doesn't mean there isn't anybody out to get me."

Following the service, we retired to the library for refreshments and mingling with all of the living presidents and ex-presidents of the United States. It was there that I had a chance to observe

President Bill Clinton, who was then in office. He was holding forth to a large crowd and had them mesmerized. We chatted briefly and then I met Hillary, whom I found smart, funny, and engaging. Clearly, they were a real power couple. President Jimmy Carter and his wife were there, along with Gerald Ford, but the only one who held a candle to the Clinton charisma was Ronald Reagan.

A very different funeral was the Paris event on January 11, 1996, officially marking the death of French President François Mitterrand while he was being privately buried in another town at a service attended by both his wife and his mistress. Mitterrand's death had shaken the whole of France. Such was his longevity in politics that hardly anyone in the country could remember a time when Mr. Mitterrand was not in public life. The Canadian contingent to the funeral was strong. Roméo LeBlanc, the Governor General, André Ouellet, the Foreign Affairs Minister and myself. We flew over on a Challenger and headed straight for the funeral at Notre Dame Cathedral.

The French newspapers were full of the details of Mr. Mitterrand's life, and not just the public part. In fact, *Paris-Match* had a special issue showing photos of the Mitterrand family, including a surprise new member – a daughter in her twenties who had been kept out of the public eye because she was the child of Mr. Mitterrand and his mistress; she had only begun to develop a close relationship with the President in the final months of his life. The souvenir edition paid significant tribute to the two women in his life and the children they produced. It was revealed that his mistress had a section in the presidential palace set aside for her family, and his wife was interviewed about the decision they had jointly reached to make public this private side of their shared life. In fact, the two families were so tied together that his wife and mistress shared the sorrow of burying him in a private ceremony that was widely reported. We Canadians had a hard time grasping it all, but our role was not to judge, merely to support and observe.

On the evening of the funeral the Canadian Ambassador to France, Benoît Bouchard, invited us to dine at the official residence. Bouchard was a colleague in the House who had begun his career in politics as a separatist but eventually became an avid proponent of a united Canada. The same could not be said for some of his colleagues in the Canadian embassy. The evening began with champagne and hors d'oeuvres in the beautiful gilded salon of the official residence. We adjourned to the dining room, where the discussion quickly turned from matters of state in Europe to the political climate in Canada. One of the diplomats in our embassy kept asking what the Canadian government was going to put on the table by way of a constitutional proposal to replace Meech. We reiterated our intention to govern without the constant constitutional wrangling that had characterized the Meech years. In fact, we shared the Prime Minister's view that Canadians were suffering from constitutional fatigue and if we could stay away from interminable constitutional discussions we would be the better for it.

At this point, and probably after copious amounts of champagne, the diplomat said it was absolutely pivotal that the Prime Minister do something to recognize Quebec's distinctiveness and announced that he was personally insulted that the Prime Minister of Canada had claimed Quebec had no culture. I was amazed that a diplomat would express such vitriol toward the Prime Minister, and realized that it was no wonder that Canada was having such a hard time getting our message heard in France.

Shortly after I returned to Canada, I spoke to André Ouellet and expressed my concern about the obvious mixed messages coming from the embassy. In his own skilful way, Ouellet dealt with the issue and paved the way for a new era in France-Canada relations. They started out badly, when our prime minister uncharacteristically disparaged the chances of Jacques Chirac getting to the top job; when he won, Prime Minister Chrétien had some skilful backpedalling to do. He succeeded so well that by the end of their respective terms, they had developed the kind of mutual respect and friendship that only two old politicos can enjoy. And the fallout from the near-loss of Canada in the 1995 referendum made that personal relationship even more important.

Lessons in Governing

Back in Canada, the work of governing carried on. As we prepared for the reduction in government spending that was necessary if we were to get our house in order, we knew we could not abandon the social side of Liberalism. As chair of the Cabinet Committee on Social Policy, I had a chance to see first-hand how ministerial initiatives dovetailed with our Liberal agendas. I also had the privilege of working with Alex Himmelfarb, an innovative bureaucrat (now head of the Privy Council Office) who was not afraid to think outside the box. He even encouraged it.

One of the first cabinet proposals for cost-cutting that I turned down was a recommendation from the Department of Health to end funding for transition houses for battered women across the country. The rationale of the Department of Health was logical; we have devolved housing to the provinces, so why are we still funding battered women's shelters? Yet Alex and I both thought this cut was absolutely crazy and we recommended that cabinet refuse the request. The amount of money involved was not huge, so I canvassed a few other departments to see if they could make up the shortfall in Health Canada's budget. No go. Health Canada was going to have to find the money and the minister, David Dingwall, was furious with me. He suggested if we wanted to stay in the transition house business, I could find the money myself. While trying to do something for the survival of women's transition houses, I had managed to alienate a friend in cabinet. The women involved would never remember, but David Dingwall certainly would.

The lesson learned? The nature of decision-making is really departmental. By the time a cabinet committee is reached, a department has already established their spending priorities. My job was really to support my colleagues, not to second-guess them. That system works well to support ongoing programs, but makes it very difficult to get real structural change. In that sense, the structural change must come at the beginning of the process. By the time the civil servants have consulted interdepartmentally (which they are required to do), a consensus has been reached bureaucratically and a minister's intervention at that point is seen more as making trouble than as making good public policy. For that to change, the cabinet process needs to be collaborative from the start.

That means agreeing on the big picture direction of the government instead of working only to support the initiatives within one department. For that to happen, we really need to re-engineer government in the same way that the private sector was revamped two decades ago. The consensus management model and the quality circles of collaboration that have revolutionized private sector management principles have not yet been tried in government. The current hierarchy in government, often referred to as the stovepipes of government – with separate vertical departments having no contact with one another – make it almost impossible to build ground-up consensus. As a result, we have a dispirited public service that questions the value of their own input, and we have politicians who are frustrated by the fact that much of their time is tied up in process, not output.

I remember once receiving an invitation in the Department of the Environment that landed on my desk so late that the event was over by the time I received it. The letter from me in response to the invitation (a letter that I never saw, and that was never sent) had been seen by more than twenty people. Each reviewed the work of another and each was editing, modifying, "adding value" to the reply letter. No one was responsible for the fact that the reply was redundant by the time it reached my desk.

When the so-called "billion dollar boondoggle" in the Human Resources Department was finally analyzed, it was shown that the error rate in public sector accounts was significantly better than that of a similar sized private sector company. But the information took a month to gather because every department and each region had its own method of collecting data. John Manley once told me that he, the minister responsible for technology, could not even collect information in his own department because the operating systems for computers within the department were incompatible. I remember trying to convince my department to switch operating systems to facilitate communication between departments; their resistance was largely due to the fact that they preferred a system where they could e-mail freely within the department, and no one outside the department could break into their system. I could not even transfer information between my Parliament Hill office and the Heritage Department because they were on different systems.

Technology should be the great time saver in government but the systems are so obscure, diffuse, and incompatible that much personnel time is used in tracking paper, not in producing creative policy. That becomes frustrating to employees who really do want to make a difference, while ministers often feel as though we are drowning in documents that mean nothing if you step twenty feet outside the Hill.

I embraced technology early on and became the first cabinet minister to use a BlackBerry. The first MP was Andrew Telegdi from the heartland of RIM (Research in Motion) technology in Waterloo. I had been using a PalmPilot for about three years when I saw Andrew with this new and fascinating technology. Right away I asked my office to get me one, and spent the next six months waiting for the department to agree. They preferred the PalmPilot. I finally went right to RIM myself to get the BlackBerry. When BlackBerry added a phone to the PDI I was thrilled. To get rid of my phone and have this new Canadian PDI made perfect sense. Instead of the device, I got a twenty-page report from the department explaining why I should not get the new BlackBerry. I ignored the report and got the BlackBerry, horrified that somebody had spent a significant amount of staff time on a report that was never used. Soon after, most department officials switched over to BlackBerry when they saw how efficient it was. There is a reason why supporters refer to it as "CrackBerry."

Another reason why organizational inertia is so prevalent in government is simple: those who do think outside the box, who want to innovate, do not necessarily get support from within the system. In fact, historically, those employees who do think outside the box, may get things done, but they also get noticed. This is not always helpful to their careers.

Fighting the Green Fight

When we advanced an aggressive environmental agenda, many of my employees were excited to really be sinking their teeth into the important issues. Yet, every time a meeting was called by the Privy Council Office to iron out a problem, the same faces would appear, and my active, keen employees would not be among them. These employees, who wanted nothing more than to see solutions to global warming, were being labelled as troublemakers by the other departments that wanted nothing more than to support the status quo. To requote my assistant deputy, he told me directly that the flak he was getting from the "centre" was going to cause him career problems, and I would be long gone, while he would be seen as a rogue environment employee who could not "get along."

A good minister of the environment makes changes, and in doing so, makes enemies. It was ultimately those enemies who speeded up my departure from the department. When I returned from the Berlin Conference, as I've mentioned, a scathing letter signed by almost every member of the so-called Friday Group ended up on the desk of the Prime Minister. Instead of hailing the breakthrough we made in Berlin, they excoriated me, accusing me of undermining Canadian interests and putting the economy at risk. They demanded that I be removed from my job.

Their predictions were very similar to those who had predicted that strengthening pulp effluent would cost us "thousands of jobs," and eerily similar to the corporate threats that "billions of dollars" would be at risk in the Canadian economy if we ratified Kyoto. Their hysteria could be traced right back to the Ministers of Finance, Natural Resources, and Justice – who talked a good game in public about being pro-environment. In fact, cabinet meetings on the subject of Kyoto ratification included hundreds of hours of briefings on why we should not ratify. Notwithstanding my keen interest in the subject and my belief that a good program of technology credits could actually make the world plan sustainable and economically interesting for Canada, I became convinced that the major discussion in cabinet was about how to do nothing. Eventually, I even stopped going to the meetings because I simply couldn't believe the horror stories that were being promoted as fact around the issue of global warming. My colleagues Charles Caccia and Clifford Lincoln were both equally frustrated at what they saw as the government's inability to move forward on the crucial issue of global warming.

On this one, the public was miles ahead of the politicians.

I remember receiving a phone call from the Prime Minister on his way to the Summit in South Africa in 2003, his last year in office. He was being briefed on Kyoto and wanted my views, as a former environment minister. I urged him to dream big, to go for it, to show leadership by being a country willing to sign on to Kyoto. A few days after his speech in South Africa he was being hammered, as usual, by an anglophone press only too willing to write environmental stories light on facts and heavy on corporate hysteria. We were visited at a meeting of the Ontario-based cabinet ministers by a PCO communications expert who was going to arm us with the facts that would help us to fend off the onslaught of criticism bound to come from a public wary of Kyoto ratification. My observation to her was that we didn't have to worry about what the corporate press was saying, the people were way ahead of them, and the Chicken Little pronouncements from people like Ralph Klein that were being widely covered by the press would have no impact on people. About a month later, I bumped into her at a cabinet meeting and she recalled our conversation, remarking how amazed she was that the Prime Minister's decision on joining Kyoto turned out to be broadly supported. In the Beltway (inside the little world of Ottawa), the lobbyists had convinced the bureaucracy that this decision would be a disaster, but it turned out to be one of the most popular decisions of the Chrétien administration. I believe his decision to move on Kyoto will stand with his decision to avoid the war in Iraq as a great Chrétien legacy. Both decisions showed that the Canadian public's capacity to discern good public policy was far ahead of the one-sided tripe they were being fed in most anglophone media outlets. And ultimately, the people are always right.

Chapter Nine

The Culture Years

The green years had been fruitful. In my time as Minister, less than two years, we had passed the toughest environmental legislation in the world, legislated the greening of government operations, introduced the first-ever national framework for endangered species legislation, banned MMT and the interprovincial transportation of PCBs, limited CFC release through the Vienna Agreement, signed a tripartite NAFTA treaty on air quality, signed a North American treaty on migratory species and, most important, signed the Berlin Agreement which paved the way for the Kyoto Accord. I left Environment knowing that, while I had certainly raised the ire of the business elite, the environmental issues were now making good progress. I wondered what challenges in the Canadian Heritage Department could be as compelling as those in Environment.

My first Heritage meeting with the Prime Minister in January, 1996, made it clear that I would not be short of challenges. He told me that it was never very popular to support the arts but it was something that defined the soul of a country and all of the arts were vitally important to Canadians. He also made it clear that he had a special place in his heart for parks, telling me the story of how he fell in love with the North and vowed to make a park for Aline, a story he repeated often about one of the high points in his forty-year career. Recalling fondly that he established more parks than any minister in history, he challenged me to beat his records. He also encouraged me to fly the Canadian flag in every part of the country, including Quebec. So I began my time with a clear mandate, to support culture and parks, even when it was not politically popular. And to ensure that Canadian symbols like our flag were proudly displayed in all parts of the country.

I was sworn in on January 12, 1996. Within two weeks, I was faced with the release of the cost-cutting budget that set us on the path to surpluses, but also cut through the heart of the Canadian Broadcasting Corporation. It did not matter that the cuts were imposed by the Minister of Finance. As Canadian Heritage Minister, it was my job to defend the cuts to the Canadian public. At one point I was being hounded by a particularly aggressive CBC reporter asking about the cuts and I suggested that the question should be directed to the Finance Minister, since he was the one who established budget priorities. Within hours, I received a phone call from Eddie Goldenberg in the Prime Minister's Office reminding me that it was my job, not Mr. Martin's, to defend the cuts. Interestingly, when the good news about CBC increases was later leaked by Finance to make sure Mr. Martin got the credit, I didn't get a phone call from anyone.

Not that Mr. Martin was ever a supporter of the CBC, although during the election campaign in 2004 against Stephen Harper he liked to pose as its great defender. This is ironic. I remember a meeting with Mr. Martin in his office when I was new to the Heritage post and very worried by the cuts my area was having to absorb.

"Look, Sheila," said the Minister of Finance, out of the blue, "if you want to raise money by privatizing the CBC, I'd have no problem with that." I just looked at him. I saw to it that the idea went no further while the CBC was under my protection as Minister.

The Shawinigan Handshake

Within days of my swearing-in, I also was witness to the infamous Flag Day ceremony that forever enshrined the "Shawinigan Handshake" in the Canadian vernacular. February 15 was chosen because it was the first day the flag had actually flown from the Peace Tower in 1965. That day I was part of a culture round table at the Canadian Heritage offices in Hull (now Gatineau) and was a little nervous because I was meeting for the first time the crème de la crème of Canadian film, people like Denys Arcand and Robert Lantos. This would be a crucial meeting since first impressions are often lasting ones. Little did I know that the round-table meeting would not be the most important thing I had to do that day.

Following an hour-long session with the filmmakers, I was scheduled to rendezvous with the Prime Minister at Jacques Cartier Park, a beautiful site overlooking Parliament, and a great location for a triumphant flag-raising planned with local elementary school students in grades two and three, a noisy, excited part of it all. I arrived a few minutes early to be briefed by a protocol official from Heritage who was enjoying her first day on the job. She assured me that everything was organized and we should have a wonderful event. But I happened to notice a few burly men gathered in front of the makeshift stage and asked her who they were. My political smell test, honed by almost two decades in active political life, told me something was not right, but she assured me that everything would be fine. The Prime Minister's limousine pulled up and he leapt out, wearing a pair of dark sunglasses. I made a mental note to ask him to remove the glasses during the ceremony and literally ran after him as he bounded up to the stage. Once on the stage and introduced by the emcee I began my introduction of the Prime Minister. So far, so good.

As soon as I turned the floor over to him, however, air horns started going off all over the park, making it impossible to hear a word he said. Finally, the Prime Minister stopped speaking in exasperation and stepped back from the microphone and whispered in my ear, "What do we do now?" "Just hang on until the master of ceremonies gets up on the stage," I said trying to sound confident. But now the crowd was pushing and shoving and we were really concerned that children were going to get hurt. All of a sudden, the PM jumped off the stage and waded into the crowd, with a team of journalists, and me, following him. I could see a phalanx of CSN protesters converging on him, blowing air horns up against him. A particularly well-known local protester got close enough to push his metal air horn against the Prime Minister's deaf ear. The PM instinctively spun around, grabbed the man by the throat, and took him down to the ground, where he was restrained by RCMP officers. I was about ten feet behind Mr. Chrétien and a few seconds later came upon this poor soul on the ground, apparently trampled in the rush. Unaware that he had been downed by the PM himself, I offered my hand to help him up, only to be told by the RCMP that he was being detained on the ground for a reason. I learned later on that he had a reputation as a professional protester although on this occasion it was not clear exactly what he was protesting against. I believe he was even paid for dental work for a loosened bridge following the fracas. In the melee, we forgot to raise the flag and it took Liberal MP Mac Harb some time to get the PM back to the stage to complete the ceremony.

And then all hell broke loose.

As I returned to my office, I received a panicked phone call from my staff saying they had seen the Prime Minister in slow motion on TV taking down a man at the flag-raising ceremony. The press was all over the story, and was going to be playing it like the outbreak of the Third World War. The PM's wife was apoplectic. The Prime Minister's Office was furious, and looking for scapegoats. The woman who organized the event asked me if she should tender her resignation after one day on the job. I said no, that this would blow over. The RCMP went to the unusual length of issuing a press statement, claiming (somewhat strangely) that security had not been breached. Contrary to all predictions, the overnight polls actually saw Jean Chrétien's popularity increase by 10 per cent and thus the phrase "the Shawinigan Handshake" was born. It was not the first time the potent symbol of the flag had provoked a firestorm, and it would certainly not be the last.

The Flag Flap

Very soon after the famous Flag Day, I began a one-year program challenging one million Canadians to start flying our flag. The political elites pilloried me, and I was denounced by almost every editorial board in the country. There was a particular backlash in Quebec where for years the separatists had successfully "repatriated" all symbols of pride, including St. Jean-Baptiste day and the Quebec Flag. My hope was to have the Quebec and Canadian flag flying side by side so Quebecers could be proud of them both. But the free flag program was also introduced at a time when most government programs were being cut, and my department did not want to have to reduce funding in other areas to supply the flags. Nonetheless, we forged ahead, and within one year more than 1,040,000 families across Canada had asked for and received a flag from the government. For many of those Canadians it was probably the only time they ever asked their government for something tangible. Even today, almost ten years after the program ended (it ran only for one year), I still receive letters from people thanking me for the flag.

I believe that the program provided a change in our culture, marking the first time that Canadians really began to become flag flyers. For years we prided ourselves on not being like those jingoistic Americans by flying flags. We were so sure of our place in the world, that leading up to the referendum we forgot that a country is not just about a cheque book. It is about our hearts. During the referendum campaign we never spoke with pride about our country, our flag, our diversity, we merely made the economic case for Canada. It came as no surprise to me that I was attacked viciously by the separatists for the program. At the same time, every instrument in the hands of the Quebec government, from restaurant menus to Crown corporation advertising campaigns, was devoted to subtly and not-so-subtly promoting the idea of a sovereign nation in partnership with Canada. It was a war of propaganda, and we were losing it. And those Quebecers who weren't separatist were too afraid to speak up in a crowd for fear of being ridiculed. The propaganda was so successful that in those days to fly a Quebec flag was strong, to fly a Canadian flag was silly.

The battle for the hearts of Quebecers was not just about the flag. It was also about the pride in being part of a bigger dream, the dream of Canada. And at the heart of the dream was culture. Culture and language were so intimately intertwined that every French-speaking Quebecer knew all the famous singers and actors in Quebec, but most of them had never been exposed to anything Canadian outside their province. The same thing could be said about the English-speakers in the rest of Canada who were unaware of the culture of Quebec. I was amazed when I became Heritage minister to discover that francophone culture outside Quebec received virtually no support from the government and anglophone activities in the arts in Quebec were largely ignored. I decided to do what I could to bridge the two solitudes.

The Jaws of the Referendum

Every Canadian who cares about our country will remember the horror of the Quebec Referendum of 1995. We almost lost the country. A few votes more on the other side and Jacques Parizeau would have declared a victory for separation and instantly started to take Quebec out of the Canada. His memoirs confirm that this was the plan. Where that process would have ended, I just cannot bear to think.

My own role in this epic struggle in the fall of 1995 was a minor one. And that was part of the problem. Here was I – someone who loved Quebec, was fluent in French, with friends all over the province, and a prominent member of the Canadian government – desperate to get into this campaign, to tour Quebec giving speeches and meeting people to get the pro-Canadian message out. Yet I, and others like me in the federal government, were frozen out. We were kept away from the greatest debate in Canadian history because the provincial Liberals, led by Daniel Johnson, insisted on running the show. "Keep out" was their message to us. "No interference from Ottawa." "Leave it to us."

One of the co-chairs of the Quebec Liberals' campaign to reject the referendum question was Liz Frulla, a former minister under Bourassa (now the Canadian Heritage minister). Lawrence Martin has recorded that "She and her team were still furious with Jean Chrétien over Meech Lake. They felt that he would only throw oil on the referendum fire, resorting to scare tactics. Such tactics might have worked in 1980, Frulla said, but after Meech and Charlottetown, Quebecers were no longer naive. 'We've had a crash course,' she told Ottawa. 'So don't give us that shit.'"

In Ottawa, the fight for Canada was largely carried on behind closed doors with no full understanding of what was really going on. By and large, most members of the cabinet believed the provincial Liberals had matters well in hand and we would be best advised to remain on the sidelines while the political rainmakers made their magic. Alfonso Gagliano, as the minister with special responsibility for Quebec would give reassuring reports on how well things were going. In fact, early in the campaign, Brian Tobin and I were the only voices in cabinet to speak out against our strategy of leaving the lead to the provincial party. I had gone to Quebec City early in the campaign to make a speech; to my surprise I found that the audience consisted of key anglophones in the community. It was rather strange to send a federal minister to Quebec to meet only with anglophones, because I knew early on that if we did not have the anglophones, we might as well throw in the towel. In any effective campaign, it is the job of the politicians to convince those who have not made up their minds, not to meet with those who are already supportive.

When I left Quebec I returned with the distinct impression that we were running a campaign for the rich, while the Parti Québécois was running a campaign for the people. Even their choice of "Yes" for the referendum question was self-affirming and positive, while we were out there peddling the "No," a negative word at best. Their slogans were ridiculed by our so-called experts, including the stylized loonie which served to remind Quebecers (falsely) that a vote for "sovereignty" did not mean they would have to sacrifice the Canadian dollar. False, but reassuring. Our experts also ridiculed the yellow flowers sprinkled among their campaign posters. Again, the flowers were sunny and warm, and left people feeling positive about a vote to break up their country. Over the years, we had even stopped talking about separation. Separation means rupture and uncertainty; instead we were now voting on sovereignty, a positive concept about allowing Quebecers to take control of their destiny, which sounded just fine. I came back to Ottawa with a sinking feeling in the pit of my stomach, deeply concerned about the referendum outcome even before the arrival of Lucien Bouchard; with three weeks to go Bouchard came in to lead the sovereigntist campaign with the phony title of "negotiator-in-chief," and instantly started to set the province on fire with his speeches. That changed everything.

Weeks earlier I had cleared off my calendar to make sure that I could spend the full month leading up to the October 30 vote travelling through all parts of rural Quebec, asking them to believe in Canada. I knew that I could be effective. Although I have Acadian ancestors, I was raised in an anglophone home in Hamilton and did not learn a word of French until I entered high school. My father spoke fluently (an Irishman from Northern Ontario) and my mom even started taking French lessons at age sixty. So when I went into rural Quebec, the first thing that struck them was how well I spoke French. Because I came from a working town I loved nothing better than to give a stump speech to convince workers they could share a bigger dream called Canada. I always loved to campaign and would think nothing of putting in a sixteen-hour day for the love of my country.

Much to my surprise, after I informed the central campaign of my full availability, the phone did not start ringing. This was a mystery. Over time I learned that the "No" campaign, headed by the provincial Liberals, had three kinds of tours: the A tour, for the people they wanted speaking throughout the province (primarily provincial Liberals and Tories); the B tour, for lesser-known lights who might be able to cover off some of the less important tour areas; and the C tour, for people they really did not want to show up in the province. I was relegated to the C tour. I found out later that invitations were flooding in from all parts of the province for ministers from outside Quebec, because organizers wanted to be able to show their regions that the rest of Canada truly did care about the outcome of this election. As soon as the invitations reached the "No" headquarters in Montreal, however, they would be cancelled or detoured to Quebec politicians. Incredibly, the "No" team was worried the presence of people from outside Quebec would actually attract votes for the separatists. At one point, I angrily remarked to one of our people, "We act as though the province is already separate and then we wonder why people want to separate!"

Let me give an example of how bad it was. I was sent in to an east end Montreal riding which was literally a stone's throw from the main "No" campaign headquarters in Montreal. I arrived with national media in tow to find an empty committee room with about six people in it. The event had all the makings of a disaster, which would reflect badly on me and worse on the campaign momentum. In the campaign office I quickly sized up the situation and announced to the waiting media that today we were going to be riding the rails – the Montreal subway system, to be exact. We left the office, made our way down to the nearest subway entrance with the six workers, and proceeded to campaign for Canada on the Montreal metro. The television clips were great, people's reaction was positive and we averted one of many near-disasters in a dismal campaign.

At this point, I was so frustrated, I went to the "No" campaign headquarters and tracked down one of the key organizers, Pierre Anctil. I told him about the near-disaster we had just been through that morning and asked him why nobody from outside Quebec seemed welcome in the referendum fight for Canada. Pierre spoke bluntly and directly. As far as he, and most Quebecers were concerned, this was a fight within the family and as outsiders (non-Quebecers), our presence would not be helpful. He then went on to say something that absolutely stunned me. He told me he did not care what the outcome of the race was, win or lose, as long as the difference between the no and the yes was not too great. I could hardly believe my ears. Imagine going into a campaign for your country when your concern for family peace overrides your desire to keep your country together! That, I'm certain, was not only the view of Pierre Anctil. It reflected the general thrust of the leadership of the "No" forces. Here we were, in a fight to the death for Canada, and many of the provincial geniuses in charge of the campaign were playing some silly tactical game of their own. So perhaps it should have come as no surprise that a smart, positive separatist campaign, coupled with internal federal divisions finally produced a near-death experience for Canada.

Only a few days before the end, the numbers on the referendum showed the separatists were poised to win. I was travelling in the west when I received a phone call from Brian Tobin. The usually ebullient Brian sounded positively shaken as he recounted the deadly numbers in the latest referendum internal polling. We were trailing by seven points. What to do? We immediately decided that the time had come to take matters into our own hands. We would let Quebecers know that we cared. And if Liberal organizers kept us out of the province, as federal MPs and ministers, we would go full steam ahead and damn the torpedoes, and organize our own rally. And so the rally that saw 100,000 people converge on Canada Place in downtown Montreal took shape in seventy-two hours. We lined up every train, plane, and taxi that could get our people in Montreal. In my own case, we sent sixteen school buses from Hamilton for a gruelling one-day round trip, and there were so many people lined up for the twenty-hour voyage that hundreds were left stranded in Hamilton. Mayor Bob Morrow organized a parallel rally to accommodate those who could not get to Montreal. Liberal MPs like Dennis Mills were pulling people in from across the country. The energy was palpable. We were positive and buoyant, sure our message was going to get through to Quebecers, who had been left wondering for weeks why no one cared.

That morning, Brian Tobin and I rose early with the intention of getting on stage about an hour before the official program, to warm up the crowd. We had already been told that, even though we had organized the rally, no non-Quebecers would be speaking as part of the official program. We knew the unofficial program would be just as important. So while mike checks were taking place, we bounded onto the stage, only to have the power disconnected by a key "No" committee organizer, to make sure we could not use the microphones. I could not believe how little so many of the organizers apparently wanted to win.

We even gave up on any semblance of an official tour. Right after the rally, we organized a small plane and Brian Tobin and I headed to the Gaspé and Sept-Îles, ending the whirlwind four-day campaign on Sunday in the Magdalen Islands. In those four days, we went from fishing village to church basement to aboriginal centre, encouraging everyone to cast their vote for Canada. I remember meeting with an aboriginal chief outside Sept-Îles on Saturday morning. Less than forty-eight hours before the vote, no one had ever bothered to contact him to seek his support; Indian Affairs Minister Ron Irwin had offered to go, but he was waiting for the okay from the "No" committee that never came. When I met with the chief and the tribal council, he told me that they intended to boycott the vote. I literally begged him to convince his people to take a stand for Canada. In the end, his people came out 7,000 strong to vote. That one Saturday morning meeting could literally have made the difference between winning and losing our country.

Yet while Brian and I were on the road, the "No" committee central campaign was on the phone in Montreal trying to cancel our visit. At one point, I received a call from a desperate local, begging us to visit their community for a final Sunday brunch pep rally. We agreed and he was ecstatic. An hour later, he was called by a member of the central committee and told to advise us we were not welcome. I won't repeat the very frank message we left for the central committee but I will tell you that the Sunday morning rally was one of the most successful of the campaign. Conservatives and

Liberals came together in the fight of our lives, the fight in which saving Canada meant much more than any political feuding.

A final word about that rally we organized in Montreal's Canada Place. Cynics may say that it had no effect, other than helping out the Montreal tourist trade. But I believe that we all owe a huge debt to the people who made the effort, and who undoubtedly swung some votes – maybe enough to win the election in that nail-biting night of October 30. So if you were among those who made the trek to Montreal, thank you. What you did was important.

As for my own role, I take it as a badge of honour that I was so active in organizing the rally in the teeth of the Johnson Liberals' opposition that they refused to let me speak there.

A Place for Aboriginals

I was always puzzled why Canadian Heritage seemed to reflect the heritage of the English and the French and ignore everyone else. The most glaring omission was that of aboriginal cultures. We have fifty-four aboriginal languages spoken in this country; tragically, most of them will disappear within one generation. The world works together to support biodiversity of the animal species, a recognized key to survival in the animal kingdom. Yet in the human kingdom, we have paid little attention to the dangers of monoculturalism and the death of diversity. What better place to start than with aboriginal peoples?

But that meant a whole shift in the culture of the Department of Canadian Heritage. Creating new programs and opening new doors often means you slice an existing pie into smaller pieces and those who have been receiving the slices tend to resist, along with their protectors in government. It took some time to convince all areas of the department – which includes sports, book publishing, audiovisual, arts, broadcasting, and much else – that this was not lip service, we had to make real changes to begin to reflect the true face of Canada. Within the space of a couple of years, we went from virtually no spending on aboriginal culture to an envelope equivalent to almost $100 million.

More important, we engaged all the Crown corporations for which I was responsible in an exercise to redefine themselves. Why was it that Telefilm Canada funded films in the millions of dollars every year and yet could not fund aboriginal films? We moved forward in every aspect of public policy and I have to say that one of the most satisfying outcomes of that exercise was *Atanarjuat* (*The Fast Runner*), a film in the Inuktitut language that took top honours at Cannes and opened the door to a whole new productive industry for the north. Even more important, a young filmmaker from Nunavut, participating in a round table on film held during the Vancouver Film Festival, told the spellbound group that one of the greatest benefits for the community was that not a single person committed suicide during the year while filming was going on. They were all engaged and supporting the production of this masterpiece, and at the same time, they were building and supporting their own dreams.

That is a dramatic example of why it is so important that heritage belongs to all of us. Why the idea that the English and the French cultures apparently were valued more than others was at odds with the basic idea of Canadian heritage. In fact, the beauty of Canadian heritage, as expressed through the Multiculturalism Act of more than thirty years ago, is that in this country your history and cultural background are valued, not assimilated, and the strands that everyone adds makes the country's interwoven fabric stronger. The idea of producing cultural diversity inside one tolerant society is the dream of Canada. And not only is it the dream of Canada. It is the hoped-for destiny of the world in the twenty-first century. Without knowing it, we are in the process of creating a framework for the twenty-first century.

In fact, two years ago, the Aga Khan, the spiritual leader of the Ismaili people, came to Ottawa to meet with ministers. He had just come from a visit with the President of Afghanistan in the hope that his Foundation could help the Afghani people rebuild their wartorn country. The President told him that what he wanted to build was the Canadian model. That encounter struck me as wonderful – neither one a Canadian, both seeing the value in what we have been able to nurture in terms of diversity. Does anyone really think that the security agenda is what will make the country safe? If anything, you only have to look to our neighbour to the south to see how governance without diversity creates walled communities and demographic ghettos. For all of that country's great achievement, a major weakness is that the right to bear arms is an underpinning of the Constitution, but there is no mention of culture.

Contrast that with Canada, where it is the role of the national government to build social cohesion, interconnect cultures, and provide the legal framework for respect for cultural differences. We now understand these "differences" as cultural diversity, now spoken of around the world as a value to be nurtured. We are even working toward a world legal instrument at Unesco which would guarantee national governments the right to nurture and protect diversity in culture. There is only one country that has worked aggressively to ensure that the instrument of cultural diversity has no legal meaning – the country which seems to believe that the security of the world is dependent on military might, while cultures and languages are something to be practised in the family but set aside when you step out into the outside world.

The Magazine Wars

My first experience with American cultural hegemony came with the so-called magazine wars. Shortly after I arrived in the department, I was confronted with an American complaint to the World Trade Organization about our tax treatment of Canadian magazines. The Americans claimed that our decision many years earlier to provide preferential tax treatment for advertising and postage rates was a violation of the WTO policy. They wanted us to offer the same treatment to U.S. magazines, and they were prepared to use every lever to achieve their goals.

It seemed strange to me that they were so intent on pursuing the Canadian magazine industry, which is really a rather small market (the source of the problems for our homegrown magazines, fighting for a share of that market against cheap international magazines) and probably not worth the attention that a WTO challenge would cause. I believed, however, they were testing the waters, to find out how much we were really prepared to stand up for Canadian culture, because their real target was not magazines but broadcasting. And they presented us with the double whammy of a WTO challenge and the threat of a Free Trade Agreement challenge.

To our horror, the WTO challenge was upheld. In fact, in the WTO decision, it was stated that there is no difference between *Maclean's* and *Time* magazine, and we were obliged to end our preferential treatment of Canadian magazines. I was appalled by the decision, appalled not only for the creators but also especially for Canadians. I decided that we had to work carefully to create laws that would fit WTO requirements, yet would allow us to support our magazines in the face of the U.S. giants.

In the Shadow of the American Machine

I remember what it was like growing up sixty kilometres from the U.S. border, where our nightly dose of television included Channel Four in Buffalo and local newsman Irv Weinstein. In those days we had so few artists and musicians that we had to scramble to televise the Junos, and the majority of Canadians had access only to a few magazines that told our stories; the rest came from the U.S. I believe that the cultural renaissance which characterized the Canada of the last quarter of the twentieth century was not an accident. It started, I think, with the arrival of public television. "Either the state or the United States" was the rallying cry that led to the formation of the Canadian Broadcasting Corporation. But even more important was the government's decision more than thirty years ago to establish a television and radio licensing system, the CRTC, that guaranteed air time for Canadian voices and Canadian stories. Equally important was the establishment in 1957 of the Canada Council, to support and nurture excellence in the arts in all parts of the country.

But our success – with Canadian authors, for example, winning prizes all over the world – did not happen by accident. It happened because we supported authors and believed in the principle that Canadian publishing houses are much more likely to plough their profits back into new Canadian writers. It happened because we nurtured a magazine industry that was crucial in linking a small population crossing six time zones. It happened because we prevented foreign ownership from swamping our newspapers, our bookstores, and our television outlets.

When I was first named minister, it was suggested to me that if I ever wanted to nurture future aspirations, all I had to do was to support the cable industry's push to lift foreign ownership limits. In fact, the editorial pages of certain national newspapers are littered with editorials suggesting I was pigheaded because I refused to knuckle under and sell out Canadian culture. Ironically, those selfsame media outlets seem to me to suffer from a conflict of interest because their cross-holdings make it hard for them to write objectively about any issues in broadcasting. How many editorials have we seen in the *National Post* castigating the CBC – or even maintaining a hostile "CBC Watch" – without the disclaimer that their sister station is actually competing with the mother corp. These same interests have worked to discredit the CRTC, despite a history that shows how much the CRTC has contributed to a healthy, diverse television and radio audience.

We may have problems with Canadian content, and there is no doubt that recent interpretations of the content rules are chipping away at our capacity to produce high-quality dramatic programming, but all we have to do is compare our situation with just about any place in the world other than the United States to see how the role of the state here has nurtured diversity. Compare our television situation with that of Greece, one of the oldest democracies in the world and fiercely proud of its heritage. Yet when they moved to a private licensing system, they did so with no government rules on content. Now, within a few short years, they import more than 90 per cent of all television programming.

It amazes me when I hear the neo-cons in Canada suggesting the government should get out of all involvement, parroting that old chestnut "let the market decide." The average Canadian child spends more time in front of a television than they do in a classroom and yet these free market ideologues reject any role for the state in overseeing what is transmitted.

The other favourite neo-con argument is the false claim that we want to build walls around Canada. That was widely repeated by those who opposed my position on the magazine wars, and it was so far from the truth as to be laughable. Eighty-five per cent of magazines sold in retail outlets in Canada are non-Canadian (read American). I pointed out many times to my American friends that if you walked into a smoke shop in Peoria and were greeted with 85 per cent Canadian magazines, people would be marching on Congress in weeks. Yet we Canadians don't complain. As long as we have access to our magazines, that access nurtured by preferential tax and distribution instruments, we are happy to welcome American cultural products into our country.

I wish we could say the same holds true in reverse.

The only area where we have been woefully unsuccessful in getting access to our own faces and voices at home in Canada is in the area of feature film. And that is the one area completely dominated by foreign product from Hollywood. The Hollywood juggernaut is a completely integrated system of creation and distribution of movies whose monopolistic practices would make Bill Gates blush. And yet neo-cons in Canada would actually like to strengthen that monopoly by weakening the few government instruments we have to reflect diversity.

The Americans just don't get it: they see it all not as culture, but as a matter of money. I remember speaking at an off-the-record round table at the Annenberg School of Communication in Los Angeles. Encouraged by the news that this was a forum of the futuristic thinkers in communication, I attended the breakfast meeting hoping to make contact with some potential American allies in the magazine wars. But the chairman started out the meeting by welcoming me and announcing that, having read my speech to the House of Commons on the magazine wars, he thought I had a lot in common with Fidel Castro. I was appalled. To fight the inane WTO decision, we had proposed legislation in the House which was WTO-proof, could not be contested, and met our objectives by making it illegal to foreigners to advertise in Canadian magazines. The legislation sailed through the House and the Senate, supported by all sides of the House.

In fact, on cultural matters, I often enjoyed a consensus amongst all members, and there was never the kind of squabbling you see on other committees. The Alliance critic, Jim Abbott, was very well versed in the area and a pleasure to work with, and Bloc critic Suzanne Tremblay was so supportive that eventually she was removed from the committee because she was deemed by her party to be too uncritical. So we had virtual unanimity in Canada – and yet all they could see in California was shades of Communism. It truly frightened me because I wondered how we were ever going to be able to protect diversity when the world's largest superpower, and greatest exporter of "cultural product" had so little interest in even understanding our point of view. It was easier to pigeonhole all of us as Communists.

On my return to Canada, I realized the only way for us to truly protect language and culture was to work in the world outside the WTO. It would only be possible to bring the Americans on side if they saw that they were isolated and in the minority. Yet to create a new world consensus without the Americans was not going to be easy. Even in the context of the magazine wars, I saw how hard it was to run counter to the wishes of the Americans. While our legislation sailed through the House and was making its way through the Senate, our own team in Washington was concerned about the impact the legislation would have on Canada–U.S. relations.

The Canadian Ambassador to Washington, Raymond Chrétien was a lifelong and respected bureaucrat who also happened to be the Prime Minister's nephew. I also worked with colleague Sergio Marchi, our Trade Minister; with a billion dollars a day of trade dependent on smooth Canada–U.S. relations, he, too, was concerned about the effect a war in this small magazine sector might have on other sectors of the economy. In fact, as our legislation moved methodically forward, the Americans threatened retaliation in the billions of dollars, homing in specifically on vulnerable big-ticket Canadian sectors, with special local attention paid to steel (directed at me) and plastics (directed at Sergio).

Eventually the issue landed right in the lap of the Prime Minister and the President. Contrary to the advice he received from the United States Trade Representative, and because of his close relationship with Chrétien, President Clinton agreed to sign a treaty recognizing Canada's right to protect our culture and agreeing to accept limitations on advertising benefits to Americans in return for us agreeing to withdraw our legislation. In the negotiations to secure a compromise, I managed to establish a $50-million magazine fund to cushion the blow of American penetration into the Canadian marketplace. In the long term, the penetration was not great, but the Americans began to realize that when it came to protecting culture, we were not going to roll over easily. They signed a treaty that was never widely publicized, probably because they did not want the Canadian exemptions to be replicated by other countries around the world. We, of course, needed the world to support us if we were going to have any hope of protecting cultural diversity in our own country.

Chapter Ten

The World Weighs In

Unesco stands for United Nations Educational, Scientific and Cultural Organization. It has the job of speaking for the world when it comes to the matter of culture. Although it has an incredibly broad mandate in world organizations, it is poorly understood – a little bit like the Canadian Heritage Department in Canada. In fact, Canadian Heritage and its fifteen member agencies had a collective budget of $3.5 billion and were responsible for the fastest growing area of job creation in Canada, the culture sector. Every day the business pages of the national newspapers were full of stories about cultural companies. And yet to most journalists, and the Canadian public, it was a department that did nothing but give out money.

I remember my first meeting with the agencies when they produced a wish list of projects topping a billion dollars in capital costs. I told them that before we spent one penny on bricks and mortar in Ottawa, I wanted to plan to interconnect every Canadian museum through the internet. I remember War Museum director Joe Guertz looking a little shocked. He was hoping to move quickly with the building of the new Canadian War Museum. But that caveat got the agencies and the department moving in a new direction. We became the first country in the world to create a virtual museums system on-line. At vcm.ca, we link our museums to the world. And I am happy to report that the brand-new Canadian War Museum designed by Raymond Moriyama will open in time for the D-Day anniversary in 2005.

Perhaps there is a reason that the power of culture in its broadest sense is poorly understood and generally undervalued. When the Aga Khan came to Canada and told us he was looking for the key to culture here, he was really speaking about the diversity we see every day on our streets: the fact that different communities can live together and interconnect harmoniously; the fact that the old wounds of the English and the French, although deep and divisive, are being healed, not through bombs and fences, but through bridges and connecting streets. The fact that our Constitution, in recognizing two official languages, guarantees that the majority cannot automatically trump the minority, imposing its will through force of numbers.

Whenever I needed inspiration for my lonely fight on culture, I had to look no further than the French Canadians, a people that struggled through oppression and assimilation for hundreds of years but managed to keep their language and culture alive in a sea of North American English. In my lifetime, there were clubs in Quebec that did not allow French to be spoken. And yet French Canadians managed to persevere and grow in numbers and in power and influence, sometimes with, but most often without, the support of governments. And I only had to look to my own ancestors, the

Acadians, to marvel at those who had resisted the pressures of assimilation and built a strong and unique culture for their children. (My Acadian ancestors came from François Gautereau, one of four brothers whose descendants were involved in the deportation from Grand Pré in Nova Scotia in the 1750s. The family name has since become Gaudereau or Goudreau or Gouthro. By the time my grandfather, born Levis Gouthro in Sydney Mines, joined up for the Great War he had become Leonard Guthro.) All of these examples were beacons of hope for other countries, countries that struggle to retain their unique languages and cultures, while participating more and more in the global community.

The world has two options, building bigger walls or building better bridges. The bridges aren't physical, they are cultural. They are about knowing each other and being confident that one culture, one language, one religion will not crush another. I compare it to the beginning of Canada, in 1864 when the Fathers of Confederation agreed to nurture two languages, two religions, and two cultures to form one country. They could have chosen to support the majority culture and ensure its domination over the other. But they did not. So when Canada was formed in 1867, it sprang from an idea that two peoples, two languages, and two cultures could live together in one country. An idea revolutionary in its time, and essential for world peace in the twenty-first century.

But what does that have to do with government cultural policy? Simply, culture is a reflection of ourselves; how we speak to each other, through words, through music, through stories. Our culture is how we nurture a baby, and how we witness death, and how we comfort the grieving. And if we don't see ourselves reflected, if our children don't hear their stories, if they see another's reality presented as their own, if they don't hear their language, then our culture, our joy of life, dies. A slow, brooding death but a death that can only weaken the world.

But what about keeping culture in its proper place, in your home, and leaving it to the marketplace when you step outside? Culture is not just about individual lives. In fact, it's an expression of the collective, the society in which you live. And if our children turn on the television and don't see it reflect the faces of the people around them, if aboriginal kids never see themselves, or their life celebrated and embraced, is it any wonder they feel like second-class citizens in the country that their ancestors generously shared with us?

So as we looked internally at our own diversity, we rewrote all the funding programs in Canadian Heritage to fill the holes in our collective consciousness that came from honouring only two cultures. And we also made a special effort to promote what we would call "interculturalism." By recognizing all kinds of different cultures in Canada multiculturalism gives us the tools we need to build our own unique, strong identities, building a stronger whole. Interculturalism helps us to know one another. We also worked with existing institutions to help them understand that promoting cultural diversity was everybody's responsibility; just because we had aboriginal exhibits at the Canadian Museum of Civilization did not mean that other institutions could ignore First Nations, Metis, and Inuit peoples. As we became more experienced in supporting aboriginal cultures, we also reaped the benefits. At the World Expo in Hanover, Germany, in 2000, our pavilion, with its strong emphasis on the stories of the North, was voted the best.

One of the challenges inside government is there is a tremendous power of inertia, which makes it very hard to change the status quo. Couple that with the top-down, ministerial responsibility stovepipes that are traditional, and it becomes very difficult to move institutions forward. In 1993, with a stroke of a pen, Kim Campbell created the department of Canadian Heritage by merging five different departments. In theory the Prime Minister has full control over what is known as "machinery of government." (And when Paul Martin came in as Prime Minister, he instantly changed one-quarter of the reporting systems in government.) Yet my experience running departments has shown me that it is one thing to change the reporting authorities for a department; it is another to build a sense of team spirit, where people will work together to support common goals. That takes time. Unlike the private sector, government often carries out wholesale structural changes in a rush, with no human resource support. No CEO in their right mind would merge five companies with no plan to unite management and establish common objectives. Yet in government, it happens often. So often, that in many circumstances, employees hunker down, hoping not to be noticed. Not being noticed as the key to survival spawns mediocrity and inertia.

As we worked to establish the conditions for interculturalism and diversity, the department became a fun place to work. We produced lots of new initiatives, including the aboriginal languages strategy, the digital content initiatives, the Canada Television Fund, the Tomorrow Starts Today investment – results of a proactive department with a great management team. Coupled with that, we worked with some of the greatest agencies whose dynamic leaders (like Jacques Bensimon at the National Film Board, Shirley Thomson at the Canada Council, and François Macerola at Telefilm Canada) made Heritage an exciting place to be. We were learning, we were growing, and especially, we were defining ourselves as Canadians. We also had dynamic partners in the artistic community. People like actor Pierre Curzi representing the film industry in Quebec and Jack Stoddart representing the English-language Canadian book publishers. Nowhere was that more apparent than when we began the fight for cultural diversity on the world stage.

Building a Global Alliance

One of the challenges we faced in culture was that notwithstanding the world reputation of Unesco, there was no international forum for culture ministers to get together to exchange ideas on an annual basis. Politicians met annually to talk about fish, finance, and farming, but never had any thought been given to establishing a world culture organization. One of the biggest stumbling blocks was the United States. Because they did not have a culture minister – and did not even understand why having a national culture minister might help them in their desperately needed bridge-building with the rest of the world – they were completely opposed to the establishment of the network.

With the support of then Foreign Minister Lloyd Axworthy and International Co-operation Minister Diane Marleau, I organized a meeting in Ottawa in June 1998 attended by ministers from twenty-two countries from around the world. We made sure that every region of the world was represented, and we worked hard to put common issues on the table. One common theme kept emerging; countries around the world were being inundated by Hollywood cultural influences with no reciprocal cultural exposure. It seemed as though the world was being viewed through a one-way mirror, and that mirror was based in America. Film industries around the world seemed to be in trouble, small publishing houses in many languages were languishing, television everywhere seemed to be overrun with American product. And many countries thought they were powerless to do anything about it.

We were able to share with them the Canadian experience. We showed them that you can fund television through a regulated system where profits are set aside to create national (in our case Canadian) content. You can develop a strong indigenous music industry by insisting that radio stations play a certain percentage of music created by domestic artists. You can make it illegal for foreign book publishing houses to take over domestic companies.

That first meeting, minister to minister, was a revelation for many countries that had already given up on the idea of protecting their cultures through legislated means. They realized that if a country as open and civilized as Canada could do it, they could, too. In this regard, we began to receive requests from other countries to supply cultural experts in fields ranging from copyright to audiovisual. The South African government used the new Canadian law on copyright, passed in 1997, as the basis for their new law. The new minister of culture from Mexico asked me to provide experts in television and film to help in the drafting of their new laws dealing with Mexican audiovisual content rules.

Culture ministers from around the world were very excited about the possibility of collaborating on policies and legislation that might help them do their jobs better. Out of the meeting in Ottawa sprang the International Network on Cultural Policy. To be a member, a country had to have a national culture minister or equivalent, which meant the United States – which always insisted that "culture" was the same as "entertainment" or "leisure goods and services" – could not join. We did, however, extend to them the courtesy of observer status, a courtesy we also extended to several international organizations including Unesco, the European Union, the World Bank, and the Organization of American States. The idea behind the Network was to engage as many countries as possible in the fight to protect cultural diversity, not just in rhetoric but also in law, as a counterweight to the growing international power of the WTO, which treats everything as a commodity.

Canada did not want to see the WTO making decisions that would limit our sovereign right to support our own culture. There were, however, elements in the Canadian government that were not too keen – and that is understating it – on taking culture out of the control of the WTO. Senior bureaucrats in the Department of International Trade made no secret of their contempt for our approach to globalization. In fact, the fierce debate divided once again on linguistic lines, with my French-Canadian colleagues understanding the importance of our cultural protective moves. Foreign Affairs, which had an overview of the world, also saw the benefits in our approach. With France as a keen ally in the battle for cultural and linguistic survival, Foreign Affairs understood the benefit of such an international body to support Canada's agenda in the world. Lloyd Axworthy was an erudite, cerebral minister who was not afraid to strike out on a path that deviated from the Americans. He had already shown his courage in pushing forward on the Anti-Personnel Landmines Treaty against opposition from Washington. Having Lloyd strongly on side made our battle with international trade much easier.

Sergio Marchi, the Minister of International Trade, had fought shoulder-to-shoulder with me in the magazine wars. This meant that he had to skate from time to time, trying to keep everyone happy, as he was also responsible for the trade flow between Canada and the U.S. But when his successor Art Eggleton came to international trade, it was clear from the beginning that he thought our approach was outdated and anti-American. He worked closely with the Americans on a daily basis and could be relied on to repeat that they were clearly unhappy with the existence of an international organization in which they had no membership.

Our second annual meeting was held in Mexico in 1999 and it was clear that the Mexican minister was walking a fine line. He lived in the shadow of the United States, which was bombarding Mexico with Hollywood on a daily basis, and he wanted to change that. At the same time, his government depended on its trade ties with the U.S. to drag it out of an economic quagmire. So when we assembled in Oaxaca, it became clear the Americans had applied pressure on their allies to try and shut the organization down.

The British were the first up to the plate, suggesting that the organization only deal with suggestions for giving out national subsidies. (Direct subsidies are allowed within the framework of the WTO.) Our work, according to them, should be restricted to giving advice to national organizations like the Canada Council and the National Endowment for the Arts, while we had no business discussing government policy. Nice try.

When that proposition was roundly dismissed by the other ministers, the Spanish delegation weighed in from a different angle. It was their view that we had far too many international organizations and we should abolish this one because they did not have time to attend all these meetings. At one point, the American observer tried to introduce a resolution proposing that we limit the mandate of the INCP. He was flatly rebuked by the South African culture minister who reminded him that he was invited as an observer, and he should simply observe.

The attempt by the Americans to kill the organization did not succeed. But we clearly had our work cut out for us if we were going to build the world momentum necessary for a legal instrument on culture to be approved outside the WTO.

The Allies Gather

At the first INCP meeting in Ottawa, we had organized a pre-meeting of cultural organizations representing over twenty countries around the globe, to analyze and review the work that we were doing. NGOs and cultural organizations had already formed their own world-wide network, intending to sensitize their respective governments about the pitfalls attached to signing on to the WTO without any regard for cultural protection. They were able to apply pressure on their governments to support the work of culture ministers and ensure that globalization did not pave the way to monoculturalism. In most countries, when artists speak out, the people listen; it is fair to say that it was the mobilization of the cultural and artistic communities, that actually killed the Multilateral Agreement on Investment (MAI). The cultural NGOs were soon joined by a newly formed international Coalition for Cultural Diversity. The first world summit held by the Coalition for Cultural Diversity was held in Montreal in 2001, with writers and other creators from some ninety countries around the world working on political action. Once again, Canadian cultural professionals in the music, film, and publishing industries were at the forefront of an international coalition of professional associations in favour of a legal instrument on cultural diversity. All this was happening in a climate where the U.S. was clearly working behind the scenes against us, but the world momentum was getting stronger.

In Canadian media circles, the francophone press covered the issue extensively. They understood the dangers of living in a society where their language and culture could be swallowed up in a sea of anglophones, and they were intrigued by a coalition which for the first time had Canada and France taking the lead together. They also saw how in this issue, the strongest of federalists and the strongest of separatists could unite. I think it fair to say that Pierre Curzi and I became fast friends during this process; when I was going through the nomination process that drove me out of my seat, one of the nicest phone calls I received was from Pierre, a devout separatist.

The English media, on the other hand, ignored the whole issue. The only time there was ever any interest was when they were commenting on my travel bills. Millions of anglophone Canadians understand that when you are living beside a giant superpower like the U.S., you have to fight every day for the right to hang on to your own identity and culture; in fact, the common language makes cultural assimilation that much more dangerous for anglophones. Nonetheless, the English media exhibited the same schizophrenia on the issue that we saw reflected inside the government in the battles between the Department of Canadian Heritage and the Department of International Trade. We were helped by the arrival of Pierre Pettigrew in trade, replacing Art Eggleton, because he brought a unique perspective as a Quebecer who understood that it would be folly to leave cultural questions in the hands of the WTO. Having Pierre as an ally in Cabinet and seeing the growing momentum in cultural coalitions at the creators' level meant the seeds I had planted by travelling the world were beginning to bear fruit.

In each country that was entering WTO discussions, the artistic coalitions were able to provide a good background for what should definitely not be signed on to in terms of cultural obligations. In the final stages leading up to the Unesco vote, we were even able to convince the Chinese to get on board. Indeed, they offered to host the 2005 annual meeting of the INCP.

Largely thanks to the work of the INCP, Unesco promised that it would accelerate the process for a legal instrument. The normal time frame for an instrument is about ten years but Director-General Koïchiro Matsuura promised the INCP executive that he would move the process forward and he did, with the support of Lloyd Axworthy. In February 2003, the executive fast-tracked the vote and in October 2003 a vote of the General Assembly occurred. The U.S. delegate spoke against the instrument but had so few allies that it was embarrassing. They realized that they were facing a broad consensus of countries around the world that feared the inexorable march toward monoculturalism, and ended up voting in favour. We had won.

Backdrop to War

All this activity was taking place against the terrifying backdrop of a possible war in Iraq. To a surprising degree the countries that were lining up with the U.S. in the move to go to war were the same countries working aggressively behind the scenes to kill the cultural diversity instrument. In the summer of 2003, I was invited by the Quai d'Orsay, (the French Foreign Office), to speak to French foreign culture officers, home for their annual summer briefing, about the importance of a cultural diversity instrument. This invitation was quite a coup because it was widely known that on matters of culture, as in other matters, the French government practiced a policy of non-interference and non-indifference with the Quebec government, which usually left Canada bringing up the rear in any discussion on culture. In this case, it was widely recognized that Canada had started the movement toward the instrument and that I had worked very closely with four French ministers, building a relationship successively with each one, the last of whom was M. Jean-Jacques Aillagon, an engaging person with more than two decades of hands-on experience in the arts; we had struck up an early friendship and worked closely on common issues.

In front of the whole cultural diplomatic community he introduced my Quebec counterpart, Pauline Marois, and myself in a way that shocked the audience. Remember, he was introducing me to a crowd that for years had seen Canada as a troublesome wedge between France and an independent Quebec, so it was natural that the response from the room was decidedly warmer when Pauline Marois was introduced. Yet M. Aillagon, part of a new government in France that wanted to make peace with Canada, introduced me warmly as his friend "Sheila" who had started the fight for cultural diversity, and introduced Pauline Marois as the deputy premier from the province of Quebec. Quebec officials were sitting up front and I could clearly see them cringe as the words "province of Quebec" left the lips of the Culture Minister. It was the first time a French minister had so clearly underscored the fact that Quebec was a province within Canada, and I could see the surprised responses on the faces of foreign affairs bureaucrats.

The panel included an author from China and a senior executive from CNN as well as Pauline and myself. Pauline Marois's statements were warmly received, while the response to my comments was tepid – until the end of the session, that is, when the representative from CNN said he saw no reason why national governments needed laws to promote and protect culture. I told the story of how our country, a stone's throw from the United States, made a decision early on to protect and promote all aspects of culture, especially by regulating broadcasting. I explained that in our country the proximity to the U.S. left us no alternative; either the state was involved, or our broadcasting system would become an adjunct of the United States'. I explained how the situation was even more serious in English because the common language and geographic proximity were a recipe for cultural annexation if we sat by and did nothing. My final comments, in support of a strong national protection for Canadians, underscored the fact that in Canada, it was against the law for CNN to buy up our television stations, and we wanted to keep it that way. This was greeted by thunderous applause from the French and they left the meeting, I think, finally understanding that the need for cultural protection is not uniquely a Quebec challenge.

We adjourned from that meeting to the Quai d'Orsay where lunch was being hosted by the French Foreign Minister Dominique de Villepin. I was seated beside him and across from British Foreign Minister Peter Mendelsohn. A heated argument erupted at lunch over the Middle East. Divisions between Israelis and Palestinians were dominating the news and the British Foreign Minister brought the discussion over to Iraq. He insisted that the Americans would be going to war, in January or February at the latest. There was no discussion about weapons of mass destruction, merely that the Americans had made their decision to invade, and so the French had a choice. According to Mendelsohn, you could be with the Americans or against them and Britain knew where it stood, and he loudly and repeatedly asked the French Minister where France stood. M. Villepin kept saying that he hoped there were alternatives to war, and that was where he believed the efforts should be concentrated. I supported the statements of the French Minister. But it was clear to me then that the British and Americans would stand together on Iraq as they were standing together against the instrument on cultural diversity. The irony of it all, of course, is that if more attention was paid to the cultures of our world, we might not be continuing an endless spiral of civil conflicts and wars between people who live side by side, but do not know each other.

Chapter Eleven

The Coronation

Shortly after the convention, some had begun spreading the word around Chrétien's office that Martin could not be trusted, that he was out to undermine the new leader." Lawrence Martin notes in *Iron Man: The Defiant Reign of Jean Chrétien*. "Not long after the Chrétien government was sworn into office, there were Martin supporters who were quietly beating the bushes on Parliament Hill in pursuit of political staff who might play a role at some future leadership convention," says John Gray in his biography, *Paul Martin*. The most unusual aspect of this long-range campaign was the role played by people who worked for the Earnscliffe Strategy Group, a company so closely involved with Paul Martin's department of Finance, as to be, in Susan Delacourt's words, "almost an adjunct of the department." She explained: "Earnscliffe was divided into two operations: one did more traditional lobbying and consulting work with industries and private sector interests; the other, the research one, worked primarily with government departments and ministers' offices. . . . The two functions made Earnscliffe powerful – and controversial."

Very controversial.

Murray Dobbin's book, *Paul Martin: CEO for Canada*, looks at the list of players at Earnscliffe after it "was sold to a handful of Paul Martin's most trusted friends and loyal political supporters when the Tories lost the 1993 election." He names David Herle, Terrie O'Leary and Mike Robinson and adds: "Over the years other Martin associates were added to the Earnscliffe roster, including Scott Reid, who worked as Martin's communications chief from the mid 1990s to 2001, and Elly Alboim, the former and very influential chief of the CBC's Ottawa bureau.

"The common denominator for those in the Earnscliffe Group was their absolute loyalty to Paul Martin and their dedication to getting him elected as leader of the party. The charge that Earnscliffe was actually working for Martin, advancing his political career more than it was working for the finance department, dogged the company for the nine years it received contracts from finance. According to the *Globe and Mail*'s Hugh Winsor, 'Mr. Herle and Mr. Alboim were clearly providing political advice to Mr. Martin, although their invoices were paid by the department bureaucrats. Mr. Herle is still providing political advice to Mr. Martin and his firm is contributing his services to the Martin leadership campaign'." (Hugh Winsor, an old Ottawa hand who knows the way things are done in the seat of government, wrote that in September 2002.)

Duff Conacher, the head of Democracy Watch, was outraged by what he saw as a built-in in abuse in the Earnscliffe-Martin link. Murray Dobbin's book quotes Conacher: "Making reference to the Lobbyist's Code of Conduct, Conacher describes how the work Earnscliffe did for Paul Martin and the Finance department is a clear conflict. 'The ethics rules clearly draw a line that requires lobbyists to choose between being a lobbyist and working for a political party or politician,' he says." When the Ethics Counsellor ruled that he saw no conflict, Democracy Watch launched a court action against him.

Certainly over time I became aware that Martin's people had set up a network of people in private companies doing government relations and with a direct line into the office of the Finance Minister. It was well-known on Parliament Hill that if a company wanted any action from the Department of Finance, they would be well-advised to hire Earnscliffe, the "government relations" experts, if they wanted to be heard. Often, with the right "hire" a company or association would get the money they were looking for from Finance, and the employee would soon be working part-time for Paul Martin's leadership. If anyone complained, there was a clear perception that they would be blackballed, and with the hand of Finance so powerful on the Hill, companies could not afford to complain. The media knew all about the links that I and the other authors quoted here have described between Earnscliffe and the Department of Finance. Some of them even knew about a private company, Lansdowne Technologies, partly owned by Paul Martin that received millions of dollars in untendered contracts from the Department of Finance during the years of Martin's tenure there. Year after year, Martin's operatives, well-placed in various government relations firms around Ottawa would ensure their priority was to solidify his position as the next leader. Yet the press, apart from the odd reference, ignored this huge story for years.

And to give him his due, Paul Martin did a fabulous job in Finance. He was able to muster national support for a major round of cost cuts while avoiding the usual collateral damage that befalls a finance minister. The beauty of his approach was that he spoke in generalities and when there were explanations to give to justify the cuts, they always fell to the line minister. Thus, as I wrote earlier, when it was time to cut the CBC, the explanation fell to me, but when it was time to increase the budget, the leak came from the Finance Department, ensuring that Mr. Martin got the full credit.

His approach was equally brilliant when it came to major cuts in health and social transfers to the provinces. Martin knew that the cuts were going to be extremely unpopular, so instead of simply cutting, he changed the spending envelope to create the Canada Health and Social Transfer, the CHST. Before he created this fuzzy transfer, there was a federal transfer specifically for health, a transfer for social spending called the Canada Assistance Plan, and a direct transfer for post-secondary education support. At the same time he was cutting the transfer money to the provinces, he changed the strict federal rules which limited their flexibility. In the area of post-secondary education, for example, the government of Canada lifted the cap on tuition costs. That cap used to force provinces to keep tuition costs within a reasonably similar, accessible limit across the country. In the CHST budget, the cap was lifted, and universities responded by increasing tuition fees so drastically that they went up an average of 110 per cent over the next seven years. While he saved hundreds of millions in potential tuition fee replacements, all the while whittling away at the average student's capacity to go to university, he also launched a series of research chairs across the country, which kept the post-secondary sector happy.

It's not widely known that he tried to target seniors. At one point, he made a serious attempt to increase the mandatory retirement age to sixty-seven. That proposal was sidelined by Prime Minister Chrétien as quickly as his earlier hair-raising proposal to abolish the Old Age Pension. His comments in the spring of 2004 on "flexibility" for old-age pensions should be viewed with some suspicion because if I know Paul Martin, his real intention is not to support the minority of workers who want to work beyond age sixty-five, but to fill the revenue gaps caused by aging baby boomers retiring and receiving a pension.

The most memorable of his attempted changes to Canada's social fabric was in that same budget. As the CHST was going to cause considerable pain to the provinces, Martin wanted to send them a few carrots along with his financial big stick. One carrot was the change in tuition fees. Another was the decision to limit federal government involvement in social programs by abolishing the Canada Assistance Plan. CAP was generous, but it also provided benchmarks for provincial spending on social benefits. The provinces wanted the money with no strings attached, which is how the CHST was designed. It also merged three envelopes in a sufficiently obscure way to make it impossible to track government spending changes on post-secondary and social programs with the same rigour as before because each province spent differently.

But the biggest carrot to the provinces was cut out of the budget at midnight just before it went to press. The carrot was a small line in the budget. It announced the plan to end the outdated Canada Health Act and replace it with something more flexible after discussions with the provinces. As Deputy Prime

Minister, I was given the privilege of reviewing the budget in advance. When I saw the reference to the Canada Health Act and the proposal to abolish it, I knew that this was political dynamite. For a Liberal government to be doing this was a betrayal of our basic principles. I went to Martin with my concerns but he shrugged them off, saying it was too late, because the budget had already gone to print.

I immediately requested a meeting with the Prime Minister, and showed him the fine print, voicing my outrage. He agreed with me, instructing the Department of Finance to take the offending words out of the budget. Jean Chrétien knew that major policy shifts like an end to the Canada Health Act should not be slipped through as budget measures. They deserved a full parliamentary debate. (Once embedded in the budget, they must be supported as confidence measures, because if a government votes against its own budget, an election is automatic.) The Prime Minister told the Minister of Finance that the budget would not be printed until I was satisfied with the new wording.

Amazingly, despite what Martin had told me, the budget presses had *not* yet rolled and within a few minutes I received a phone call from Deputy Minister of Finance David Dodge. He wanted my home fax number. A rewritten copy of the budget came through on my machine just before midnight. The offending words had been removed, but it was clear the fight for the Canada Health Act had only just begun.

Fast forward to the election of 2004. Prime Minister Martin is musing about raising the retirement age, his Finance Minister, Ralph Goodale, is publicly warning about the collision course expected in the current health-care system and his Health Minister, Pierre Pettigrew, is publicly musing about the necessity of providing more flexibility in Medicare. Pettigrew's honest mis-statement, echoing comments already made by the Deputy Prime Minister, begs the question: Where are the voices of dissent in the Liberal Party? Where is the moderate wing that can bring the Party back to the centre, the place where most Canadians expect to find the Liberal Party?

Add to that the inexorable march toward military integration with the United States, embodied in the prenuptial agreement already being negotiated for the Son of Star Wars — although, of course, we are assured that nothing is being decided, no, this is not really the weaponization of space, and so on. Where is the Liberal Party? What happened to the values of Lester Pearson and Pierre Trudeau when the Leader gives up on the United Nations in favour of a new, restricted membership to be determined in concert with the United States and other "like-minded countries"?

The Democratic Deficit in the 2003 Leadership Race

Any leadership race is expected to produce a healthy debate. In this case, the debate was traded in for a coronation. A coronation based on the fact that the party leadership, convinced they were backing a winner, did their best to ensure that no debate took place. The members of the once-proud Liberal Party trooped into a leadership race with a preordained result and no debate of ideas. With the same systematic single-mindedness that he had applied to taking his shipping company to the top, Paul Martin made sure that no one would challenge him.

Money played a large part in this. "The sheer scale of fund-raising would have shocked Martin's father," says John Gray in his book, going on to give examples of large contributions. "With Martin accumulating that kind of money, it was hardly surprising

that some of the other contenders in the race to succeed Jean
Chrétien simply dropped by the wayside; it seemed like an invitation to spend a lot of money for no particular purpose."

That money bought a huge machine. Murray Dobbin notes
that "Martin had between twenty and twenty-five paid staffers
working in campaign offices in Ottawa, Toronto, Montreal, and
Vancouver as early as December 2002, one full year before the
leadership convention."

In the final days leading up to the leadership vote, he had
squadrons of people working full-time under the guise of various
lobbying companies with links to him and/or Earnscliffe. And he
had infiltrated every area of the Party to the point where senior
officers were prepared to trade away democracy for the chance to
be close to the action.

To get the delegates he wanted, the Party's membership rules
were deliberately corrupted. The club system – genuine Liberal
clubs could legitimately elect delegates to send to the convention –
was gerrymandered to the point that in one province alone there
were so many phoney clubs that a total of twelve people elected
sixty delegates to the convention. If you were supporting Martin,
you could break all the rules. But if you dared step out of line by
supporting another candidate, your club would be delisted, with
no legitimate course of appeal. John Manley's son, who headed up
the Liberal club at McGill (which has been around for a few years)
saw his own club disqualified on a bogus charge simply because
the majority were backing the wrong horse. My own brother had
a ballot snatched from his hands in his home riding in Montreal
when it was discovered he was related to me.

It was ruthless, it was undemocratic, and it was highly
successful.

It was highly successful because the media had already decided early on that the debate was not even worth covering, and because the Party itself structured the debate to ensure that the front-runner and putative new leader was never exposed to a real test. For example, they organized the debate seven months before the leadership vote. They fixed the questions so that each candidate was limited to three minutes on issues handpicked by regional caucuses, all of them controlled by the Martin group. We actually spent more time in the Liberal leadership debating Placer mining than we did missile defence. Health care was accorded a total of three minutes per candidate. The debate format was undemocratic and yet there was a giant cone of silence within the Party about a format that crushed the kind of healthy debate that should take place in any leadership race. The leadership race is the best chance to test your best ideas within your own family. Better to test them amongst Liberals than to wait until the election to discover what you stand for. But the Martin group had quietly put all the pieces in place to ensure that nothing dangerous like new ideas interfered with their coronation.

The policy chair, Akaash Maharaj, a bright, erudite, multilingual consultant, was a real believer in the power of ideas. He had been campaigning for more than a year for the position of party president, based on a platform of inclusion and empowerment. The Martin group knew he had developed a powerful network, particularly among minority communities, so they approached him to signal he would have their blessing to run for president, as long as he played by their rules and organized a very early debate, with the aforementioned limits on real discussion. Akaash acquiesced, even though a little part of him wondered. Sure enough, after he had finished the dirty work in limiting debate, he received word shortly before the convention that he was no longer the chosen candidate. Instead, the Martin group would be replacing him with Mike Eizenga, a photogenic, well-spoken lawyer from London, Ontario. Akaash was crushed. He told me that he even considered quitting the Party, so discouraged was he by his own shortsightedness and by the fact that he had been duped. I encouraged him to hang in there, arguing if all the people who believe in ideas leave the Party, where will we be? He defiantly went ahead and ran for the president's job anyway. Despite the huge push by the Martin forces for an Eizenga coronation, Akaash apparently lost by only about forty votes. "Apparently," because of course they never did release the vote count.

I refused to give up the fight. I knew that I faced certain defeat, as one by one other candidates came to the conclusion that a win was impossible. But I believed the Liberal Party was about more than winning. It was worth fighting for. We were fighting for those who cannot fight for themselves, fighting for those who don't have a voice at the table, fighting for those who need a champion. I remember one day early in the campaign meeting with a group of organizers in Ottawa. One of them happened to be a young man by the name of Ragge, a leader in the Somalian community. He told us the story of how their young people live within a stone's throw of Parliament and yet might as well be a million miles away. His friends are doctors, architects, lawyers – educated people who emigrated to Canada, believing in the Canadian dream. Ten years later, they are the cab drivers and the office cleaners, wondering when their time will come. Twenty years ago, I raised the issue of foreign credential recognition in the Ontario Legislature. And today, those doctors still cannot practise, while in Canada our people are desperately short of doctors. I knew the race would provide an opportunity to hear their voices. I knew their Canada was worth fighting for.

Ragge was like thousands of others who over the years have shown me the value of public service. During the nomination battle in Hamilton, a woman came to the door in a modest apartment building. When she saw it was me, she ran out and hugged me. "You don't even know me," she said, "but twenty years ago, when I was in trouble, I couldn't even put food on the table, and you were there to help me. All these years have passed and I always wanted to say thank you. I have never been involved in a political party but now it is my turn. I will come out and vote for you."

Let me give a local, Hamilton example of a fight worth entering. We are going through a huge struggle in our community now as the largest employer, Stelco, tries to get bankruptcy protection and squeeze pension funds from retired Stelco employees. Many of those workers put in four decades, working in the most difficult, even hellish conditions, and now their employer, aided by a change in provincial pension legislation made by the Mike Harris government, has underfunded the pension fund and left them in a state of financial limbo. Those pensioners are worth fighting for. And yet what do we get? Talking points from Prime Minister Martin's office suggesting that we can't get involved, it's a private sector matter. A whole community in shambles and the Party that I always thought would be there for the workers is missing in action.

To try to provoke a debate I produced a policy document called "Foundations: An Action Plan for Canadians." The twenty-page plan, guided by the incredible talent and skill of Dr. Brooke Jeffries and Charles Caccia, costed every single promise and laid out a blueprint for a Canada where every Canadian would build on their potential. The plan called for strategic investments to build stronger communities and to create economic development in all parts of the country. I called for revitalization of our infrastructure and real investment in green innovation. I laid out a road map to solve the growing problem of a country where, increasingly, rural and isolated communities are populated by seniors and children, and where young people migrate to the eight cities across the country that now include the majority of Canadians. The plan tackled the issue of recognition of international credentials, it proposed a new partnership for the regions and aboriginal communities. I unequivocally supported human rights in all forms, including the rights for gays and lesbians to be treated equally in all aspects of the law, including marriage. I provided a blueprint to guarantee a return to affordable, accessible university education. A complete section was devoted to a critical investment in public transit. I promised to open up the equalization formula which has doomed some provinces to remain forever under the financial gun. No waffling for me, no notwithstanding escape clause that permitted me to say one thing in front of one group and the opposite elsewhere. It was a substantive piece of work which really looked at Canada through a new lens.

Foreign-Policy Concerns

All the elements of a great liberal debate were included in the Action Plan. On foreign policy I raised the question whether Canada is best protected by participating in a security perimeter around North America or by building bridges with the world. And the need for a real public discussion about whether Canada should enter into a Son of Star Wars nuclear missile defence system with the United States was obviously a key component. In the lead up to the leadership vote I became increasingly concerned about Paul

Martin's approach to Canada's role in the world. Would we continue as an honest broker in the world, as the country whose earlier Prime Minister had been a partner in the establishment of the United Nations Peacekeepers? It worried me that although Martin was not in cabinet when the decision was made to remain out of the war on Iraq, some of the most vocal caucus proponents of our participation in the war were his key people. These pro-war voices that ended up in the new Paul Martin cabinet included the Minister of National Defence, David Pratt. David was his early adviser on all things military and I remember having a heated discussion with him before 9/11 when he produced a paper saying it would make a lot more sense for the Canadian and U.S. Armed Forces to be integrated for continental defence. I told him Canadians would never agree to integration because it would basically spell an end to any pretence of Canadian sovereignty in relation to international military matters.

What could not even be contemplated before 9/11, however, became common fodder for the security agenda in the aftermath. In the same atmosphere, limitations on civil liberties that would never have been tolerated became commonplace. The (to my mind extremist) "perimeter theory" proposed by Tom d'Aquino and his big business lobby was wholly embraced by Martin. Under the Pratt proposal our military integration would be complete, and obviously economic and social integration would follow closely. It would certainly be impossible for us to maintain our own sovereignty and, I fear, we would never be able to make the kind of independent decision that, for example, we made to stay away from the Iraq war.

There is no doubt in my mind that if Paul Martin had been the leader, we would have gone to Iraq with the United States.

A Liberal Course

My hope was that the leadership race would be the opportunity for these major defining issues for Canada to be debated. It would be a chance for Liberals to set us on a liberal course. The great strength of the Liberal Party was that it always managed to keep the government on an even keel. The leadership debate would allow the Party to be the ballast on the keel of the Liberal ship. The presence of young people in huge numbers meant that the corrective measures that needed to be taken for the future would be articulated by them first. The resolution on same-sex marriages, for example, came from the Party first. The push for accessible tuition fees came from the Party first, the decision to ratify Kyoto came from the Party first.

The beauty of Jean Chrétien's style of leadership was the way he always knew when to correct the direction on the Liberal ship of state. He moved early to send Canadian troops to Afghanistan, permitting us to be directly and helpfully involved in world security while staying out of the war in Iraq. He refused to send troops to Iraq, but refrained from the kind of high-level anti-American rhetoric that left France vulnerable. His ability to steer the ship while keeping an even keel was vastly underrated. But soon after his departure, Liberals and Canadians began to see a Liberalism that was no longer balanced. In the early attack ads prepared for the 2004 election, Canadians were warned: "If Stephen Harper was Prime Minister last year, Canadian troops would be in Iraq this year." "If Stephen Harper becomes PM you'll have two health care options. Be rich. Or don't get sick." You could just as easily have substituted the name "Paul Martin" for "Stephen Harper" on both counts.

Paul Martin knows as well as I do that the American Nuclear-Missile Defense system (NMD) is not popular with Canadians. That was why he was so careful in privately moving ahead with negotiations while publicly reassuring Canadians that no such negotiations were contemplated. No need to debate, especially if the debate would unveil deep divisions between the position taken by the elites and that of the people. His refusal to bring this key question – involving nuclear weapons in space – to the people reminded me of the fatal statement from Kim Campbell that elections were not the right moments to debate policy.

Political leadership conventions are great opportunities to debate the ideas framing the next decade of governance. In fact, for many Liberals, they are the only opportunity. We have been in government for more than a decade. During that time, ordinary Liberals have not had the same influence on public policy as they do when we are in the Opposition. In government, as I've described, ministers work directly with departments in the formation of policy, and often the direction of a department or even a government is quite different from the collective views of its rank-and-file members.

It is absolutely simple for the NDP to reflect totally the views of its members. They have never been in government nationally and have never had to test whether their views fit the larger challenges of governing. The Conservatives have not governed for a long time, and the new Conservatives and the Bloc Québécois have never served in government. In the case of the Bloc, it is their expressed goal never to serve as the government of Canada. Against that backdrop, it is much easier for each of those parties to speak only for rank-and-file members. Hence, the only party with a long history in government that has continuously had to balance the views of its members with the views of the total population is the Liberal Party. That makes our leadership debates that much more important because it is the only time when the potential leaders, and their beliefs, are answerable only to the members of the party.

Clearly, in our Party, the ordinary members are more small 'l' Liberal than the country at large. Hence, the legislation on same-sex marriage was handily passed at a Liberal convention while getting a brutal ride in the caucus of the same party. Any opportunity for the ordinary Liberal members to have their say is restricted to national policy conventions, usually held every two years, and leadership conventions.

Contrary to what the newspapers would portray, leadership campaigns are not just about personality clashes – the so-called Chrétien-Martin fight, the Chrétien-Turner split or the Turner-Trudeau division. There are many key and emerging issues which the party faithful can pronounce on at these conventions, thus giving the leadership a feel for where the Liberals are going in terms of our policy direction. If the country is uneasy about nuclear missile defence, for instance, or our growing integration with the United States in security matters, is it not better to test these themes during a debate within the Party than to bury them in the hopes they will disappear – only to see those same questions forming the major themes in the election campaign?

But in the coronation of 2003 no such debate occurred. Even the media decided early on that this was the race that wasn't. In fact, when my policy document was launched, the main comment in the French media was on the type of paper it was printed on. In the English media there was far more coverage given to Belinda Stronach's fashionable wardrobe than there was to the Liberal leadership contest. But, to be fair, that was not the decision of the media. It was the decision of the Martin team when they resolved early on to avoid all debate. They even hoped to avoid a vote by fixing the rules and ignoring the opportunity for healthy renewal that offers itself up in any leadership debate.

"The campaign" as Murray Dobbin put it in his book, "looked more like a hostile corporate takeover than a genuine party contest."

I signed up thirty-two thousand new members to the Liberal Party during this period. The vast majority of them were from minority communities experiencing their first opportunity to participate so directly in the democratic process and the openness of the Liberal Party. From Newfoundland, where I discovered a small Sikh community meeting in a home while they were building their gurdwara, through to British Columbia, where an incredibly diverse team of volunteers worked tirelessly to build support for their chosen candidate, these were all future long-term members of the Liberal Party. Win or lose, I was a team player and they were getting their first taste of political life in Canada, and loving it.

In addition to these thirty-two thousand new members, I had supporters who had worked on my first campaign (dating back to 1977) and friends and allies with whom I had built close personal and philosophical ties over the past two decades. We were ready for a great debate of ideas. We never expected to win, but we believed it was important for the Liberal Party to tackle the tough issues of the day. We knew the Conservatives, true to their name, would always work to conserve the status quo, which too often means working for the privileged few. We knew the NDP was too tied to single interest groups to really make the kinds of breakthroughs they needed to reflect all the people. And we despaired of a Bloc that had only one agenda: destroying Canada. So we worked day and night.

The policy team was superb, and the regional organizers and volunteers were enthusiastic and devoted. While Paul Martin had approximately two hundred paid employees on the ground, our total payroll could be counted on one hand. The media could have played their usual role of putting the front-runner under the microscope. Instead, they seemed far more focused on ensuring that no candidates actually ran against Mr. Martin. The *Ottawa Citizen* was particularly incredible. When Ralph Goodale accidentally under-reported $180 million in government funding paid to Mr. Martin's private companies, that was a "clerical error" buried on the inside of the paper. When my assistant, Charles Boyer, had an expense account with breakfasts averaging fourteen dollars, that made huge front-page headlines, and a complete inside page was devoted to dissecting his expenses. I found it interesting that the figures on Charles Boyer's expenses were available right down to the penny, but the Martin company monies were rounding errors in the millions!

The media have always thrived on scoops. They need the inside story. When Martin was in Finance, he helped to make the careers of certain favoured journalists by leaking information at the ideal time for his purposes. He worked hard through Earnscliffe to ensure that his media contacts were up to date and a good scoop would often be rewarded by a favourable headline. Even when he left Finance, and especially during the latter days of the leadership campaign, he would utilize his extensive network to leak bad stories about colleagues and then reinforce them through comments from his political operatives throughout the country. After many months of this treatment, people like Herb Dhaliwal in his riding and John Manley in his leadership campaign had had enough, and finally decided to get out. I vowed to stay in until the end, and stick it out I did. I thought it was the most painful six months of my life, but I did not know what Martin had in store for me next.

Building to the Convention

The internet is an incredible source for recruiting new, motivated people. The beauty of our organization was that the team was spread throughout the country and not concentrated in a few urban areas. Through the internet we were also able to communicate with each other at reasonable cost, which created a sense of teamwork linking old and new Liberals from coast-to-coast. One of the commitments I made early on to the team was that if they joined me, I would not quit before the end. When Allan Rock and Brian Tobin both decided not to enter the race, they left many loyal followers uncertain what to do. In the case of one poor fellow, he had started with Brian then switched to Allan, and then he was about to give up on the whole process; I convinced him to join my team and told him that he could be guaranteed that I would not leave the race before the end. I kept my part of the bargain, even though I was harassed and hounded at every turn by those who thought I would serve the Party's interest – a.k.a. Paul Martin's interest – by leaving.

For weeks I would wake up in the morning to screaming newspaper headlines predicting my departure. It was even widely written that I was in the race only as a favour to the outgoing Prime Minister. The same journalists who covered rumour after rumour after rumour as fact never even bothered to read the policy document that formed the basis of my platform.

Frustrating, yes. But exhilarating, too, because I had a chance to connect with a whole new generation of Liberals from every corner of the globe and to reconnect with Liberals in small towns and villages scattered throughout the land. Some of those connections even started on the internet.

Amongst the most touching of the messages I received was an e-mail that moved me to tears as I read it for the first time on the eve of the ides of March. It came from Saiorse Akasha and read ". . . from a kid who admires you. I am not sure if you'll get this or read it. I doubt you will – you're probably really busy. I just want to tell you that I loved your speech at the convention in November. I have heard my dad put you down without being able to say why he doesn't like you – though I suspect it has something to do with him being sexist – and I have told him off again and again, demanding that he be able to explain his opinion or go and inform it a little better. At the convention, one person who was sitting beside me whispered at the end of your speech "well, all the queers are behind her, anyways," and I was shocked. It was something I'd expect to hear from my fellow students in my high-school classes – not from an intelligent person attending a Liberal convention. Once again, I found myself telling someone off and demanding what it was he felt you were missing." She wound up saying, "I want you to know that I hope you never give up. I hope you get through this thing and show the world that Canadians are better than Paul Martin's people assumed when they decided on this immature course of action. You have a point to prove and it's one I happen to like. Even if society is not ready to accept it yet, I hope you at least make enough of a point so that when my generation or the next come to take our turn at bat, it will be. I loved your speech. It reminded me of all the things I've believed in since I was a six-year-old kid watching all my friends turn on me because I befriended the weird girl who walked funny, and holding my ground despite the loneliness and the cruel, mocking words. I admire people who hold their ground for human rights, for integrity, in just the way that you are doing."

The speech that she spoke about was probably the finest one I have ever given. The tension was high. The great bridge-builders in the Martin team had squeezed us in between the coffee break and lunch on the second morning of the convention. They even refused to open the doors to accommodate the hundreds of people standing outside the room trying to get it. It took the feisty Claudette Bradshaw to force the Martin organizers to open the room up to allow in those who wanted to hear me speak. The room was very small, of course, because the Martin forces negotiated it that way. Nonetheless, I had the outgoing leader on one side with his wife, Aline, and their daughter, France, and son-in-law, André. On the other side, I had Paul Martin and his wife, Sheila. I was brought in to the music of Susan Aglukark singing the beautiful chanson "O Siem we are all family." That set the stage for a speech that was designed to do two things: build bridges between the outgoing government and the incoming one, and lay out a blueprint for the future success of our Party and our country.

My family sat proudly in the front row; from my mother, who had witnessed the year of pain that I had gone through, to my sisters Mary and Brenda, and my brother, Kevin. My siblings knew the hard side of politics. My husband, Austin, knew how hard it was going to be. He reminded me to look over to him if I felt stressed and he would make me smile. And he did. My children and grandchildren were there. My stepdaughter Jackie, who was about to give birth by caesarean, even made sure her due date came after the convention. They were all there. My mother was like a lioness, wanting to protect her cubs, especially her fifty-year-old daughter cub, Sheila. She was so upset at how we had been treated through this whole process that she wanted nothing more than to give Paul Martin a piece of her mind. I reminded her of the family rule she had always preached: the test of good manners is good manners in the face of bad manners. They had all seen the glory but most especially the pain of the past year. But they wanted to be there to support me in what they knew would be a test of fire. Simply getting through this weekend was going to be a testament to my character.

My whole family had been privy to the farce that the Liberal Party characterized as Super Weekend, the weekend voting two months earlier to choose the delegates to the convention by binding them on the first (and only) ballot. They all participated in a leadership vote that would have been thrown out in any third world country. The vote was spread over three days with interim announcements on how the counting was going. The Martin forces, by pure coincidence, arranged for all their strong ridings to vote on Friday, and ensured that we sent our strongholds to the polls on Sunday. The team of David Herle-Karl Littler had organized an elaborate strategy to discourage the wrong people from voting. MPs were actually encouraged to remain in the polling stations, hovering over voters as they came to cast their ballots. In one riding in Ontario, they even created a separate line for non-white African-Canadian voters, ostensibly so they could help them with the voting. This occurred after the MP had sent a form to the home of a leader suggesting in their language that if they supported me they would never again be helped by the constituency office.

The Martin team had so gerrymandered the voting system that in Nova Scotia a total of fewer than ten people actually managed to elect sixty delegates. Bogus clubs were rampant but when we complained about them, our complaints were shunted aside. All this stuff wasn't just the usual nomination shenanigans between excited organizers. It was widespread, organized fraud directed from the top. In Saskatchewan, Martin organizers parading as party officials ensured that all nominations were skewed to ensure the outcomes. There was the old trick of holding the delegate selection meeting several hundred miles from the Copps support base. But in areas where that wasn't enough, they disqualified hundreds of voters for no reason, and then were actually seen giving out fifty-dollar bills to ensure their voters showed up at the poll. Another, more sophisticated approach, widely used across the country, was to ensure that the returning officers did not initial the Copps ballots, so they would be thrown out on the count. In some areas where no Copps scrutineers were present, they magically managed to get a 100 per cent voter turnout and every single person voted for Paul Martin. My own brother had the ballot torn from his hands in Notre-Dame de Grace when it was discovered that his name was Kevin Copps.

I know that, barring accidents, there was no way on God's green earth that I could have been successful in a two-person race with Paul Martin in 2003. But I also know that if the Martin executive had not ridden roughshod over the democratic process, the voices of small "l" liberals in the party would have ensured that the party remained in the moderate centre. On the Friday night of the vote to select delegates, we were running at about 15 per cent of the vote, so imagine my surprise when party officials announced that my vote was below 10 per cent. British Columbia and Alberta were bright spots, since in both we managed to capture almost one-third of the vote. Our final tally, after all the shenanigans, was 13 per cent, but that total, too, was buried. In the end, many of our delegates could not afford the thousand dollar fee to register at a convention when the outcome was already predetermined. Instead, they came as observers or volunteers, and the Martin forces were then able to crow that they received over 90 per cent of the vote.

And crow they did. At every Liberal convention since Confederation, the winner has graciously brought the losing contenders to the stage. Not this time. I was not even allowed up on the stage when the winner was announced. Instead, I was wedged into a small corner of the Air Canada Centre with my hardy band of supporters, and even that small area was almost taken over by Martin bullies. At one point, the now "Honourable" Jim Karygiannis (and I use the term advisedly) came over to try and kick our delegates out of the Copps section. Jimmy K. is a huge man and he used his weight to push around Kieran Leblanc, a female supporter of mine from Alberta who weighs all of about 100 pounds. Other Copps supporters intervened and Beatrice Raffoul finally got the MP and his henchmen to leave, but there was no doubt that his actions, verbal and physical, were nothing less than assault. All this happened in full view of the Martin organizers, who did nothing. (You'll never guess who showed up at the "showdown in Steeltown" that marked my nomination meeting. The selfsame heavyweight member named a minister by Mr. Martin as a reward for his long years of throwing his weight around. Lawrence Martin's book reminds us that "Jimmy K's" political career involved "tough-guy helpers" with names like "Heavy Stick" and "Two-by-Four.")

The final evening at the Air Canada Centre was strangely quiet, given all the attention paid to getting a great start for the new leader. Bono gave a fine speech but the crowd was strangely tentative. Thousands of Liberals were still reflecting on the words of Jean Chrétien the night before, who left the Party with some parting words of wisdom that are worth repeating. He urged the new Leader never to underestimate the intelligence of the Canadian people and always to remember to be a Liberal. I think I detected a certain sense of unease that all was not well in the great Liberal family. Many of us understood that at the core of Liberalism was a fundamental commitment to democracy, to giving a voice to the underdog, to hearing the less popular voices, to ensuring that no one was left behind in the great dream called Canada. The stampede to a coronation saw the Liberal Party lose the very value that we are sworn to uphold, the value of democracy.

Chapter Twelve

The Business Liberals

I joined the Liberal Party in 1977. After almost three decades, I thought I had begun to understand the reason the Liberal Party of Canada was the most successful political party in the democratic world. We had formed governments in almost the whole of the twentieth and early part of the twenty-first centuries. When Conservative victories happened, their time in power tended to be brief. We had managed to capture the secret to success in Canadian politics. A large part of that success was ensuring we represented the broad spectrum of Liberalism, from the small 'l' New Democrats in a hurry to the fiscal Conservatives. Keith Davey, "The Rainmaker," often opined that the secret to the Liberal Party was campaigning from the left and governing from the right. We gave the Canadian public conservative budgets and liberal social agendas.

The recipe certainly seemed to work. In the latter days of the Chrétien time in government, some of our most controversial moves, including same-sex marriage and a broad decriminalization of marijuana, were wildly popular amongst certain segments of society and unpopular amongst others. Those with whom the decisions were popular tended to be small 'l' Liberals and women. In the caucus there was a distinct split between men and women in support of both initiatives. In fact, it tended to be women who carried the torch in caucus on social issues. Bonnie Brown, as chair of the social policy committee, and Paddy Torsney, a small 'l' Liberal, both represented very conservative ridings yet managed to thrive, notwithstanding their very liberal views. Generally speaking, the Conservatives who vehemently opposed our initiatives were unlikely to be voting Liberal anyway. In our own caucus, however, we had a group of evangelical MPs who lobbied ferociously against both the same-sex marriage and the marijuana legislation.

Every Wednesday morning we would gather in the caucus room, a beautiful hall with vaulted ceilings on which were painted pictures of working families from all parts of the country. It was a constant pictorial reminder of the reason we were all there, to support the families who help our country grow strong. On the walls, the families were early twentieth-century vintage, with no blended families and certainly no mommy and mommy families.

But inside those four walls in free-ranging debates MPs spoke with passion and conviction. Some believed that same-sex marriages would destroy society, or that decriminalizing marijuana was the slippery slope to crackhouses. Chrétien was always wily. He gave everyone their say, never expressing disrespect for a point of view he disagreed with. But in the end, he almost always came down on the side of Liberalism. Just as his instincts were unerring in Iraq, so he understood that those who saw the twenty-first century through the prism of equality would support a law that said the state had no place in the bedrooms of the nation. A simple concept, incarnated almost forty years earlier by Pierre Trudeau. Chrétien, a devout Catholic, also understood that the state should be free to establish contract law which did not coincide with the rule of the Church. In fact, in the climate following September 11, to many of us the importance of separating church and state became even more relevant.

When Paul Martin took over the Party, I thought he would have the wisdom to understand that balance. I may have doubted his sincerity in some of his policy postures, but I always believed that he would want to win. Having worked so hard to get there, he would know that history showed him how to win. I should have been wiser. Several years earlier, I had hosted a dinner party for a small group of people including two of Paul Martin's close associates, David Herle and his life partner Terrie O'Leary. Our dinner at the Ritz on Nepean in Ottawa was delicious. The conversation was lively and we were all having a great time – until we started talking politics. To my amazement my fellow Liberal David Herle started to attack Mr. Trudeau and Mr. Chrétien in the same breath, claiming that they were destroying Canada. Then Terrie started in on Mr. Chrétien, with equal venom. Fresh from her $200,000-plus appointment to Washington by the government, she railed on about how Mr. Chrétien and his gang had done nothing for her and her people. Then she asked me, "What about your people?" "You may be surprised," I replied, "but most of 'my people' are in politics because they believe the Liberal Party can make a difference, not because they want something for themselves." This was not well received. The dinner ended shortly after that and I filed away the negative conversation as a bad memory.

Paul Martin in Power

When Paul Martin finally came to power, he had a chance to shape the party in his image. And it was the image that David Herle had evoked that night that stuck in my mind. Martin's cabinet was certainly a reflection of his loyal campaign team. That was as it should be, because many of his most loyal followers had been working for more than a decade, or in some cases, almost two, to secure the leadership for him. Some were newer to the Martin fold. Agriculture Minister Bob Speller, a star on Mad Cow, BSE, and some of the issues faced early in the Martin mandate, had actually worked for me in the previous leadership campaign. But it was also fair to say that the team was largely made up of Martin loyalists who also happened to represent the right wing of the party.

One of those self-described "business Liberals," who stated on television that he did not knock on peoples' doors during campaigns was Tony Valeri. Tony came to Parliament in 1993 and very quickly established himself as a "business Liberal." Early on in my time as minister for the environment, he showed up in my office with an acquaintance of his who was in the waste management business in New Jersey. The man in question, Frank Battaglia, was subsequently killed in a car accident. His family had developed an interest in the Hamilton airport and Tony was in my office to see if I could come up with $70 million to invest in Mr. Battaglia's operation. He claimed the money would be used to improve the environment. I informed him that since we were in the middle of a major cost-cutting exercise, I could not provide him with the money he was seeking. I also asked him to provide a business plan for all the wonderful environmental things he intended to do with this money, a plan I never received.

That week, I was at the Liberal Christmas party. It was a huge event, including over two thousand of your closest friends, Liberals and lobbyists, held annually at the Ottawa Congress Centre. When we were in the Opposition, we held the party in Room 200 in the West Block, a warm, intimate place for a party that truly was a gathering of friends. In government, we went with friends and met many Ottawa area–Liberals as well, but so many lobbyists were present, it was difficult to make your way to the bathroom without being stopped and asked for a government grant. In this case, we were at our table and received a jeroboam of champagne. I looked over, and it was none other than Frank Battaglia giving me the nod and smile that went along with his champagne. I smiled and sent the champagne back.

Tony did not have much to do with me after that, although we would see each other every week at the caucus meeting. Over the course of the next decade, there were really only a couple of times when his work garnered national attention. Once, when he accepted a free trip to the Superbowl as a member of the so-called Liberal Beer Caucus. The second time was when he managed to set up a meeting with a terrorist organization while he was attending a WTO meeting in Beirut. This questionable record meant that he was hardly a candidate for the inner circle of national decision-making. However, two days before Paul Martin formed the cabinet, it became obvious why Tony was there. As a cabinet minister, Tony would be a tougher opponent for me to fight in a nomination race.

The leadership convention came and went. For the first time in the history of the Liberal Party the leader not only openly attacked his predecessor, he ignored his opponent. The morning after the Air Canada coronation speech, he called a caucus meeting for 8 a.m. Again, he missed an opportunity (I assume deliberately) to even acknowledge my hard-fought campaign or the thirty-two thousand people who actually joined the Liberal Party because they believed in my ideas. On the contrary, his eternal spinners made it very clear that he had won with such an overwhelming majority that he did not need to build any bridges. He actually had himself believing that the numbers he quoted at the convention (over 90 per cent of the party) were real. He believed that with that kind of backing, anyone who was not with him was against him, and the only way they could be dealt with was by a purge. The persistent phone calls and messages I received made it very clear. Get out or we will get you out.

I visited the Prime Minister-elect in his Confederation Block office the Saturday morning before the cabinet was announced. He was smiling and cordial, but I could tell by his body language that there was no room for me on his new team. We started with idle chatter about our Christmas plans. We then talked about the culture file and shared some views on western alienation. All the while, I could tell he was beating around the bush because he did not have the guts to look me in the face. Instead of telling me straight out that I would not be part of the new cabinet, he kept broaching the subject of "an appointment." I answered quickly, telling him I was not interested in any patronage appointment. At fifty-one years of age I was far too young to retire to the diplomatic world. Besides, I wasn't that diplomatic.

When he urged me to keep my options open, I looked him in the eye and said, "Paul, I don't know how much clearer I can be. I do not want an appointment. I went into this race for the leadership because I had things to say about the future of our country, not because I was looking for a soft landing. You choose the cabinet, and if there's not a place for me, that's entirely your decision. All I ask of you is that you get Tony Valeri to run in his own riding." "Ah, that is a local matter," he said, and shifted the subject to something else. No specific offer was ever made to me. (I subsequently learned that even though he claimed the Hamilton East Stoney Creek fight was strictly "a local matter," he signed over the presidency of the association to Chris Phillips, Tony Valeri's campaign manager, more than one month *before* a vote by more than three thousand people in the riding chose Henry Lee instead of Chris.)

"We Will Make it Impossible for Her to Win"

The Wednesday before the cabinet was chosen, David Herle contacted a close friend of mine to pass along a message. "Tell her to take the patronage appointment because on Friday, we will make it impossible for her to win." Just how impossible I did not comprehend at the time. But sure enough, Friday came and my opponent in the nomination battle was named to the inner cabinet, one of only eight people in Canada, and also named to the powerful Transport portfolio. "Lucky for me," I thought, "he'll be criss-crossing the country in the cabinet while I'll be able to get down to the real business of politics, knocking on the doors of as many Liberals as possible, asking for their support."

And so the recruitment drive began. And recruit we did. We had an incredible team. My long-standing riding president, Henry Lee, had retired as a school teacher the previous spring, so he devoted his considerable time and energy on a full-time basis to building the team. We had so many fine people, and amazingly they represented all the diverse communities in Hamilton East. Gucharan Dhaliwal, Tejinder Singh, Charanjit Thind from the Sikh community, Sovann Pao from the Cambodian community and Aslam Dar and Sardar Khan from the Pakistani community, as well as longtime riding association members like Marie Nault, Christine Guitard, and Cremilde Cowles, and many more. From Mary Kiss, a longtime, well-respected alderman to Sam Merulla an outspoken current councillor, we had a dynamic, diverse, and energetic team. In spite of the party's limitations on memberships, we were literally turning them in at the rate of almost 100 a day by the end of January.

Karl Littler insisted on holding the Hamilton East–Stoney Creek battle amongst the earliest nominations and he also made sure that it took place on the same weekend as the Mississauga–Springdale fight between Carolyn Parrish and Steve Mahoney. These two nominations proved to be the largest in the country, so why do you think Littler wanted them both on the same weekend? It was simple. With our sale of memberships, we had secured 6,600 members in good standing of the Liberal Party. My opponent had sold 4,400 memberships. With those odds, in a fair fight, we were well on our way to victory. But this was to be no ordinary fight.

Paul Martin, who publicly pretended that this was all a "local matter," out of his hands, was so involved in directing the outcome that on the twenty-sixth of January he signed a letter to Elections Canada stating that the new riding president of Hamilton East–Stoney Creek was none other than Tony Valeri's choice for riding president, Chris Phillips, as I've mentioned earlier. The only problem was that the actual vote to determine the president did not occur until the fifteenth of February. So one month before the vote, the leader of the party had already informed Elections Canada of the outcome. When we were planning for the founding meeting where the president would be elected, our opponents told us openly, "Look, we don't care if you win the association presidency, because the leader will get rid of the president anyway." I did not realize at the time that his intention had already been filed in writing with Elections Canada. So much for the democratic deficit.

Littler, whose "sharp elbows" are mentioned by Susan Delacourt, also controlled the location of the meeting. In most ridings, it is the president who determines the location, in consultation with the campaign teams. But in this case, they chose the location over objections lodged in writing about the site in question. In a riding with a registered voters' list of eleven thousand they held the meeting in a school gymnasium that was sharing the 325-car parking lot with a field hockey tournament and a public library. I had lined up a shopping centre with ten thousand parking spots and plenty of space but I was informed in writing that because there were three doors in the area to be utilized, it was unsuitable. The Cardinal Newman gymnasium location had seventeen doors. Perhaps our opponents had plans for those extra doors from the start. In fact, we have television footage of an official with the Liberal Party, Ashley Dent, actually ushering Valeri voters in through a secret entrance, and then angrily demanding that the television cameras filming the illegal entry be switched off.

The day of the meeting was Kafkaesque. We estimated that up to a thousand of our people were turned away at the doors. At one point, I was told by the fire department that I had to leave because there were so many people waiting in the corridors that it was a fire hazard. We estimated that five hundred more ballots were counted than the number of people who voted. At one point, the chief returning officer made a surprising ruling that all uninitialled ballots counted. Later, people found marked ballots stuffed in garbage cans. The voting system was so chaotic it was impossible to match the number of people who voted with the tally. At the end of the day, one of my volunteers who had emigrated to Canada from Afghanistan confided to me that he had seen elections run more democratically in his home country.

While the Permanent Appeals Committee at the Liberal Party of Canada was supposed to be reviewing our case, we collected over two hundred statements from those who observed serious irregularities at the polls and signed statements about what they experienced and observed.

I am sorry to say that I was not surprised by the dirty tricks. I had seen them first-hand during the leadership and so I knew what to expect from Karl Littler and company. What did surprise me was how blatant they were. Liberal Party rules require that completed membership lists be delivered seven days before a nomination meeting. Our list arrived at approximately 11:30 p.m. the night before the vote, with almost four hundred names deleted. Names like senior citizen Frank Caldwell, who joined my provincial association in 1977. There was clearly a strategy to target senior citizens, apartment dwellers, and those with family names originating from Asia; coincidentally, I had strong support from those same groups. Not only were hundreds of names deleted from the lists at the eleventh hour but the meeting itself was set up to ensure a maximum amount of chaos. The ballot boxes were sitting in the middle of the room, secured by scotch tape while party officials milled around, clustered in groups. The media was not allowed in the room, nor was I, except to vote, and we were entitled to a grand total of twenty-two counters and five floaters to oversee a voter turnout expected to be in the thousands.

It was a disgrace. Longtime Liberal and Order of Canada recipient Jimmy Lomax stood in line with his wife Susan for four hours only to be told that after years of loyal party membership, his name could not be found. (Ironically, the same people whose names were "not on the lists" all got invitations to the Valeri victory party, when their names mysteriously reappeared.) Jimmy, a local steelworker and hero who organizes the annual Christmas drive for children at the local hospitals, subsequently went public to say he was so disgusted with the Liberal Party's role in this nomination fiasco that as a lifelong Liberal he would be voting NDP the next available opportunity. He was not alone. The provincial by-election held following the death of my friend and colleague Dominic Agostino saw the NDP fortunes soar to 65 per cent of the vote while the Grit vote plunged.

I had little hope the current Martin leadership in the party would give me a fair hearing on appeal, but my lawyer advised that if I wanted to get justice through the courts, I would first have to file an appeal within the party system. So I paid my thousand dollars and filed an appeal. The Appeal Committee was a lot less interested in the facts than in an agreement in which I would stop speaking about what went on. In fact, they asked me to sign an undertaking that I would never speak about the appeal, and I would give up my right to any court challenge in return for having a hearing on the facts. They also asked me to sign an undertaking to cover all legal costs for the lawyer hired by the Party (John Campion) and a lawyer for Mr. Valeri. My lawyer estimated the potential legal costs at a half a million dollars, with little chance of a fair outcome. He said he had never seen a deck so stacked in a process that is supposed to reflect fairness. It was so bad that I was literally being wheeled into the operating room following an attack of kidney stones, when the Party appeal committee chair Robert Peck informed my lawyer by e-mail that I had twenty minutes to sign the Party's secrecy agreement or they would simply throw out my appeal. When he was advised that I was in the operating room, his sympathetic comment was that I had had plenty of time previously to consider the issue.

Following my lawyer's advice, I chose to withdraw my appeal from the Party process because I did not want to be subject to a code of silence, as this very frank book demonstrates. I am pursuing the appeal process through Elections Canada, and there is a police investigation ongoing regarding irregularities in the campaign. I am a firm believer that the truth is more important than a cover up, and that is why I broke the Liberal code of silence to write this book.

I did not do it without a full reflection on what my decision might mean for me. I have been a member of this party since I ran in my first election in 1977. In the party, as in a family, dirty laundry is usually kept hidden. Everyone knew that the leadership rules were rigged. Everyone knew what was going on in the party. Everyone knew that my nomination bid was rigged to lose. But I was urged to keep it in the family. To break away, to go outside, is breaking the Liberal code. I remember David Smith putting his arm around me and saying, "You are such a trooper," before a press conference when I laid before the public the rottenness of the process. Some friends and colleagues shake their heads and ask why, why am I pursuing this? In fact, the day of the press conference when I announced my appeal, one of the members of the press asked me, "What about the members of the Liberal Party, what will they think?" It was at that point that I held aloft – as the book's cover shows – the more than two hundred sworn statements alleging fraud and said, "*This is* the Liberal Party." Ordinary people do extraordinary things for our party because they believe it to be the best vehicle for democracy in Canada. Not because they are on a government contract, not because they are a paid lobbyist, not because they are seeking personal gain. But because they believe the Liberal Party can be the instrument to change Canada.

My unerring belief in the core democratic values of Liberalism remains. What remains to be seen is whether Liberalism and Liberals still belong together. Business Liberals are an important part of our party. But they are not the whole. In fact what energizes me is the chance to be the voice for those who do not have a voice. When I finally penned my retirement goodbye to the people who believed in me for twenty years, I tried to capture the real challenge in restoring Liberalism.

Dear friends,

I never thought I would be writing a letter to you signing off as the Liberal Member of Parliament for Hamilton East. Unfortunately, for reasons that most of you may have read about, I will not be running for the Liberals in the upcoming election. Today is not a day to dwell on the reasons why. History will judge those better than you or I. My tears (and there have been tears) are bittersweet. Bitter because I would have loved to continue to serve you. Sweet, because the twenty years you have given me have been an incredible journey of discovery. Discovery of myself, my Hamilton, and my Canada. Hamiltonians are a tough people. Making steel does that – it makes you strong and I know you will weather the future challenges ahead for steel. Like steel, Hamiltonians are real, what you see is what you get. We are not chi-chi or café latte, we are donuts, cannoli, and samosas. I have always tried to reflect you in my time in Parliament. YOU. Not the bosses, not the big money. The ordinary person who needs a strong voice. I know there have been times when I have let you down. I know there have been times when we have disagreed.

But throughout the past twenty years, I have tried my best to fight for you. Today I have included a list of some of the important projects we have worked on together. The most important of these is the new vision for the Hamilton Harbour, a people place where we can proudly bring our friends and neighbours to show them how beautiful Hamilton is. The second is the World Road Cycling Championships. We finally saw ourselves as the world should see us. A green, beautiful friendly place to raise a family.

The list also includes some of my accomplishments for Canada. Wherever I travelled, around Hamilton or around the world, I promoted our city as a microcosm of how the world should be. People living together. Different religions, different languages all living on the same street. All getting along, realizing that when one is strong we are all strong but when only one is strong, we are weak. From the churches to the gurdwaras, from the mosques to the temples, we can be strong if we work together. If we work for all, our community will grow and prosper. I hope and pray that this will not be my last letter to you as a Liberal MP.

Today I am turning the page on a chapter of a book that is not yet fully written. With your help, we will complete the book together.

Sheila Copps

Epilogue

It is the day after Canada Day. The flags are laid away for another year. The acrid aftermath on the ground is all that remains from the glorious firework showers in the air. This was the first year in many that Canada Day was not a working day for me. With no command performance on the Hill and no speeches to deliver, I could simply relax and enjoy my family. And enjoy I did. Canada Day coincides with the birth of my first granddaughter, born to Austin's daughter Jackie and her husband, Tommy, three years ago. During those three years, I have been so busy travelling the country that I have not had as much time as I would like to be a gramma. So her birthday was a great chance to kick back, relax, and realize what is really important in life.

The day was also a chance to reflect on the cliffhanger of an election that in the end produced a minority government led by Mr. Martin. To be watching my first election since 1977 as a spectator was a different, uncomfortable experience. My energy is still boundless, so I made a vow to campaign for Liberals across the country, notwithstanding my deep animosity toward the current leadership. When people asked me why, I replied: "I'm a Liberal. Always was, and always will be. Do I agree with everything that happens in my party? No. But I still believe our approach, the moderate one, is the best way to build Canada."

I campaigned in fifteen ridings across four provinces, hoping to elect Liberals who could keep the government honest. The campaign was a roller coaster because the first four weeks saw Paul Martin's team run away from the record that had made the Liberal Party the most successful political organization in the world. They had started off their mandate in January by demonizing former colleagues and actually firing people – good people – from their jobs. The parade of dismissals, not to mention the strange things that went on at nomination meetings across the country, left party members feeling bruised and vulnerable. Confusion reigned and Liberal popularity plummeted. The Martin gang had spent ten years scheming to take power away from Jean Chrétien; once they actually had it, they seemed to have no idea what came next. A party that had the support of the majority of Canadians went into a free fall, with the Paul Martin team losing twenty points in popular support in the first months of 2004. The actual election date – which should, in my often-expressed opinion, have been held off to the fall – was delayed and delayed and delayed, leaving the impression that the Prime Minister was a ditherer who could not make up his mind.

When the writ was finally called, we got a very clear picture of what Liberals were against but little vision of what we were for. The campaign seemed based on the premise that people would vote for Paul Martin if they thought he was not a Liberal. Canadians saw a lot of why we should not vote for Gilles Duceppe, Stephen Harper, or Jack Layton. We saw very little of why we should vote for Paul Martin. Ironically the two reasons we should not vote for Harper, health care, and the war on Iraq probably raised more questions than answers. Jack Layton was quick to point out that when the Liberal government had to make a decision on Iraq, Mr. Martin did not speak. Those of us on the inside knew that he had been working very hard to get Prime Minister Chrétien to join the Americans in the war. Likewise on health care, the message was clearly Liberal while the messenger was not. When the so-called social issues came to the fore in the campaign, it was ironic to see Paul Martin fighting hard for equality in same-sex marriages when he had worked just as hard in caucus to ensure that same-sex marriage was not supported. Other ironies will occur to people who have read this book.

Senator Keith Davey had always advised the Liberals to campaign from the left and govern from the right. In the dying days of the campaign, it was the shift back to the centre – greatly assisted by the right-wing Conservative voices speaking up – that actually saved Paul Martin. Stephen Harper's first mistake was the press release that accused the Prime Minister of supporting child pornography. That was so absurd as to test the credibility of the Harper team. Harper followed that mistake by his ill-advised public musings that he might actually form a majority government. The attention immediately shifted away from the shifting sands of the Liberal campaign to the huge questions surrounding the merged new Conservative Party, and the right wingers who seemed to be signalling that big social changes were on the way once they got power. In the end, the public took the advice offered by former Tory leader Joe Clark. "Better the devil you know than the one you don't." (And Joe, significantly, actually campaigned for Anne McLellan, helping her to a narrow win in Edmonton for the Liberals.) Martin limped to victory with a weak mandate. No clear majority emerged as the public clearly wanted to keep all political parties on a short leash.

The next two years will be a fascinating chapter in our country's story. The voters are always right. This time, once again, they achieved the goal of Liberalism with limits. They found the centre, I believe, because that is where Canadians feel most comfortable. And they addressed the real democratic deficit by putting power back into the hands of Parliament. As a spectator, I will be watching with great interest and making my opinions known.

The first signal that Paul Martin has learned his lesson will be what happens with missile defence: was he really serious when he said that, unlike Harper, who simply wants to sign on to the U.S. weaponization of space, he would chart an independent course for Canada? Was Gilles Duceppe really serious when he said this vote had nothing to do with the separation of our country?

As a Liberal, I will be waiting for the real values of our party to re-emerge. It's not enough in politics to know what you are against. To inspire, to lead, to build, you have to know what you are for. I'm for a Canada of real equality, where each region, each person feels included. A Canada where linguistic and cultural diversity is celebrated. A Canada where every girl and boy, Singh, Smith, Chan, or Copps has an equal chance in life. I hope you can share these beliefs, and my belief that the principles I have discussed in this book are indeed worth fighting for.

Acknowledgements

I wrote this book myself, so am happy to take any credit – or blame – that comes with its publication. I wrote it from memory. Obviously, too, any relevant meetings or conversations that I had are described here as accurately as I can remember.

I am grateful to the other authors whose books I have quoted here: they were extremely useful. Obviously I checked my recollections with others as often as I could; I am very grateful to them for their helpful contribution. But I stand behind everything I wrote, even if it makes me unpopular in some quarters.

Books don't write themselves, so I want to thank all those who put up with me while I was locked away writing it, remembering my previous career as a journalist. Special thanks go to my family, all of them, for their support, but especially to Austin and Danelle, who had to live with me.

Sheila Copps
Ottawa, August, 2004

OTHER TITLES FROM
DOUGLAS GIBSON BOOKS

PUBLISHED BY McCLELLAND & STEWART LTD.

ON SIX CONTINENTS: A Life in Canada's Foreign Service 1966-2002 by James K. Bartleman
A hilarious, revealing look at what our diplomats actually do, by a master story-teller who is a legend in the service. "Delightful and valuable." *Globe and Mail*
Autobiography, 6 x 9, 256 pages, hardcover

RUNAWAY by Alice Munro
The Atlantic Monthly in 2002 called Alice Munro the "living author most likely to be read in a hundred years." This collection of eight superb new stories shows us why.
Fiction, 6 × 9, 352 pages, hardcover

TO EVERY THING THERE IS A SEASON: A Cape Breton Christmas Story by Alistair MacLeod, with illustrations by Peter Rankin
Almost every page of this beautiful little book is enriched by a perfect illustration, making this touching story of a farm family waiting for Christmas into a classic for every home.
Fiction, illustrations, 4⅝ × 7¼, 48 pages, hardcover

HERE BE DRAGONS: Telling Tales of People, Passion and Power by Peter C. Newman
The man whose books on politics, business (*The Canadian Establishment*) and history have sold two million copies tells the most fascinating story of all – his own life, from child fleeing the Nazis to editor of *Maclean's*.
Non-fiction, 6 × 9, 736 pages plus photographs, hardcover

DAMAGE DONE BY THE STORM by Jack Hodgins
The author's passion for narrative glows through this wonderful collection of ten new stories, ranging widely in time and space.
Fiction, 5⅜ × 8⅜, 224 pages, hardcover

DISTANCE by Jack Hodgins
"Without equivocation, *Distance* is the best novel of the year, an intimate tale of fathers and sons with epic scope and mythic resonances. . . . A masterwork from one of Canada's too-little-appreciated literary giants." *Vancouver Sun*
Fiction, 5⅜ x 8⅜, 392 pages, trade paperback

Here I am greeting
Boris Yeltsin.

Representing Canada
as Minister of the
Environment, helped
by Charles Caccia (left)
and Clifford Lincoln.

Austin lays a friendly
hand on President
Clinton as Prime
Minister Chrétien and
I pose for the camera.

With Hillary
Rodham Clinton.